FIRST FIND THE COURTHOUSE

An Anecdotal History of
the 83rd Judicial District of Texas
from 1917 to 1995

by
Mary Katherine Metcalfe Earney

Mary Katherine Metcalfe Earney

LISTO
PUBLICATIONS

To my girls,
Ann, Emily Anne, Genie, Joan, Judith

And my boys,
Craig, Frank, Trey

For their constant support

Library of Congress Catalog Card Number
97-76574

ISBN: 0-9660550-0-4

Listo Publications
P. O. Box 35038
Houston, TX 77235-5038
713-721-3003
713-721-7272 (fax)

Acknowledgments

Many people gave their help through the years while I gathered this material. Bob McLaughlin of Alpine, a long-time court reporter of the 83rd Judicial District of Texas, was especially helpful. Members of the Trans-Pecos Bar Association patiently answered my questions and listened to my experiences as did Judge Lucius Bunton and Judge Alex Gonzalez, last judge of the old 83rd.

County district clerks of the six counties were considerate and patient, especially Ramona Lara, Presidio County district clerk; Hazel Carr, Reagan County district clerk; and Peggy Robertson, Jeff Davis County district clerk, now county judge of Jeff Davis County.

Writers could not exist without librarians. I am grateful to Ester Sanchez and Natalie Mellard of the Marfa Public Library and Meleta Bell, archivist of the Archives of the Big Bend, Sul Ross State University, Alpine, Texas. Betty Dillard, researcher, Alpine, Texas, helped me fill in details of the 1980s.

Representative Pete Gallego was always gracious about sending me legislative information from Austin. Thanks also to Representative Mike Krusee of Taylor and his secretary, Barbara Lorraine.

C. M. "Fritz" Kahl of Marfa talked of many events and was a much appreciated cheering section.

Many thanks to the great, good people of the Wesleyan Retirement Home in Georgetown, Texas, who faxed, copied, cut, and smiled for me many times--Helen Hampton, Deborah Basquez, Jovita Cook, Mary Gurley, Juanita Apple, and April Bryce.

And my heartfelt gratitude to Miriam, Rosario, and Robert Halpern, who assured me over and over and over again that I could write.

In fact, the residents of the whole, wide Trans-Pecos area were their usual outstanding selves. To all of you, I give my thanks.

83rd Judicial District of Texas

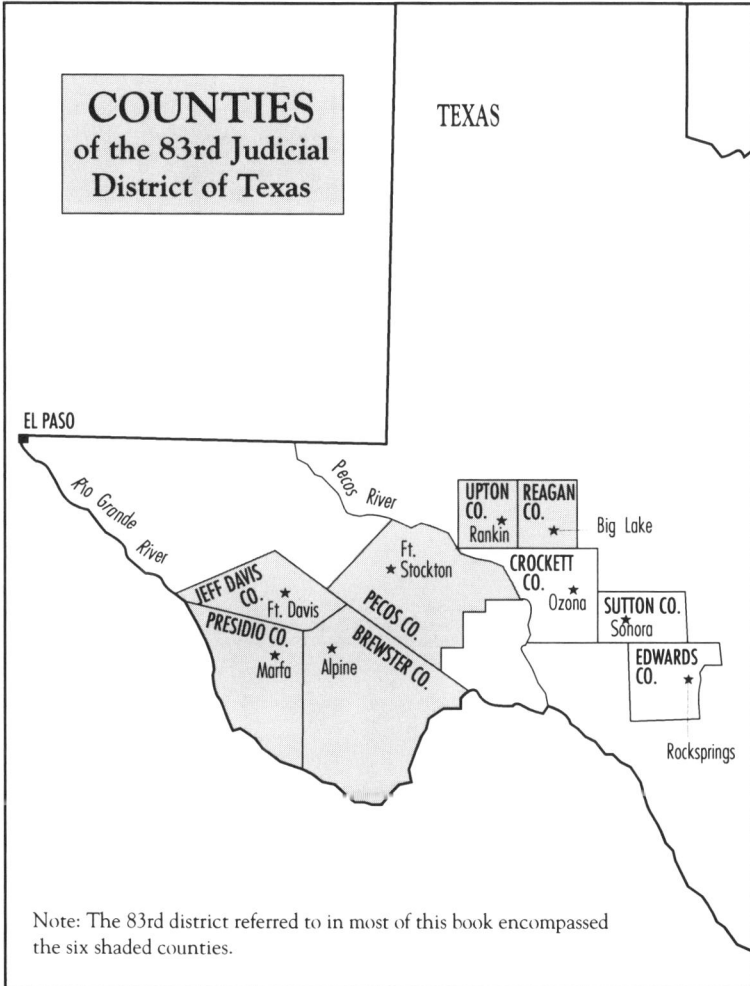

COUNTIES
of the 83rd Judicial
District of Texas

TEXAS

EL PASO

Rio Grande River

Pecos River

UPTON CO. ★ Rankin

REAGAN CO. ★

Big Lake

Ft. ★ Stockton

CROCKETT CO. ★ Ozona

JEFF DAVIS CO. ★ Ft. Davis

PECOS CO.

SUTTON CO. Sonora

PRESIDIO CO. ★ Marfa

BREWSTER CO.

Alpine

EDWARDS CO. ★

Rocksprings

Note: The 83rd district referred to in most of this book encompassed the six shaded counties.

In 1917 the 83rd Judicial District of Texas consisted of Edwards, Crockett, Sutton, Reagan, Upton, and Pecos Counties.[1]

In 1925 it consisted of Jeff Davis, Presidio, Brewster, Pecos, Upton, Reagan, Crockett, and Sutton Counties.[2]

In 1929 it was changed to include Jeff Davis, Presidio, Brewster, Pecos, Upton, and Reagan Counties.[3] This is the six-county district represented throughout most of this book.

In 1995 the Legislature redrew the boundaries of the 83rd once again. Reagan, Upton, and Pecos Counties now make up the district. Brewster, Culberson, Hudspeth, Jeff Davis, and Presidio Counties are in the 394th Judicial District.[4]

Judicial Districts

District	Dates	District Judge
Pecos County	Organized 1875	Charles H. Howard
20th	1876-1880	Allen Blocker
	1881-1884	T. A. Falvey
34th	1886	T. A. Falvey
41st	1887-1891	Winchester Kelso
	1892-1899	Walter Gillis
	1899-1903	J. M. Goggin
63rd	1904-1908	B. C. Thomas
	April 1908	W. Van Sickle
	November 1908-1916	W. C. Douglas
	1917	Joseph Jones
83rd	May term 1917-1922	James Cornell
	1923-1940	C. R. Sutton
	1941-1947	Hunter O. Metcalfe
	1948-1952	Alan R. Fraser
	1953-May 1954	J. C. Epperson
	August 1954-June 1972	C. E. Patterson
	August 1972-1984	William H. Earney
	1984-	Alex R. Gonzalez

Source: Files of the district clerk's office of Pecos County, Fort Stockton, Texas.

Table of Contents

Foreword

Texas's 83rd Judicial District has more stories than can be put into a single book. They are as varied and as full of human emotion as the people they are about. In this book I have chosen to concentrate on the judges of the old 83rd and some of the highlights of their terms of office.

If those stories seem to be colored with unofficial comments, it is because I knew the judges, ate with their families, and laughed over funny events with them. Not only did I grow up in Marfa, Texas, my father was Judge H. O. Metcalfe and I grew up to marry Judge William H. Earney.

The court has always been an integral part of my life, and I would like to share some of its fascination with you.

Mary Katherine Metcalfe Earney

Chapter 1

A Little Further than Nearer

"How near to the murder victim were you?" the lawyer asked the witness.

"No muy lejos, ni muy cerca, pero poquito más lejos que cerca," he replied.

"So, you were a little further than nearer," the attorney said. "Is that right?"

The man nodded his agreement.[1]

This bilingual exchange happened in the Presidio County Courthouse of the old 83rd Judicial District in Southwest Texas. The man's response on the witness stand was a perfect description of the district, a little further than nearer to the rest of the United States.

The judges of the old 83rd were traveling men who covered some 19,539 square miles in the Trans-Pecos of Texas.[2]

There were six courthouses, six district clerks, and myriad people of all flavors, including ranchers, farmers, oilmen, wildcatters, aliens from Mexico, and local citizens with strong opinions. Because of this variety, courtroom sessions had an aura that swung between television's *Night Court* and the courtroom of dignified Judge Hardy of the old Andy Hardy movies.

Of the six counties in the district, Brewster, Jeff Davis, Pecos, and Presidio were in the western half of the Trans-Pecos while Reagan and Upton were east of the Pecos River, cattywampus (a real, Southwest Texas word) to the other four. The Trans-Pecos area lies west of the Pecos River, north to the New Mexico line, and south to the Mexican border--the Rio Grande.

The geography of the counties included the chaparral and the flattop mountains of oil-rich Reagan, Upton, and Pecos Counties, then stretched south to the Big Bend National Park in Brewster County, west to the fertile Presidio Valley of Presidio County, and north to the rolling Davis Mountains in Jeff Davis County. Stark mountains perch beside deep canyons; rolling, grassy plains; greasewood and cactus; abrupt rimrocks; barren lands; spring bluebonnets; and oil rigs. Dry arroyos give stark contrast to the Rio Grande but a short distance away. Everywhere you look, stretches of lonesome highways guide the eye to the horizon miles away.

Many a lawyer, new to West Texas, ruefully remembered laughing when his first law professor said, "The first requirement for being a successful lawyer lies in finding the courthouse." The memory, while pleasant, was no longer a laughing matter as he sped over the fifty lonesome miles between the towns of Pecos and Fort Stockton.

The standard comment of lawyers new to the area was, "How was I to know that Fort Stockton is the county seat of Pecos County? And how could I know that the town of Pecos is in Reeves County and not even in the district?" With six courthouses to find, many found it confusing.

From the first judge who gunned down his man in true John-Wayne style on the dusty streets of Del Rio to a more recent judge who lost his pants in court, each brought his distinct personality and set the tone for his court sessions. The lawyers were no less interesting, and attitudes toward the legal community continue to run on an opinion continuum that ranges from indifference to deep affection.

As an example of the indifference, when asked what his father did for a living, one little boy replied, "Oh, nothing. He's a lawyer."[3]

For affection, we have the story of Juan Dominguez of Marfa, who early one Sunday morning ran across the Presidio County Courthouse lawn to the house of attorney H. O. Metcalfe.

When Metcalfe came to the door, Dominguez sobbed, "Oh, Mr. Me'caf, my wife, he [sic] just die, and now all I have is God and you. God can't help me; so you will have to do."[4]

In turn, the legal community accepted two absolutes for the district. First, if there was a shooting in a bar on a Saturday night and there were fifty people in the bar, forty-nine will have been in the five-by-five rest room at the time of the shooting. Second, the deadliest shot in the district is an angry wife who has never shot a gun before, standing outside in the dark of the moon, aiming a .25 caliber pistol at her husband, who is running away from her as fast as he can. Lawyers say with a knowing smile and a wink, "She'll drill him every time."[5]

Many legal codes have set the rules for the Trans-Pecos, with a variety of cultures blending into the unique present-day system. The laws of the nomadic tribes of the area evolved into the laws of the Indian tribes. After tribes possessed horses and guns, Indian law demanded that no firearms be fired in camp. Other laws of the frontier adopted by the settlers included "The first man to touch a stray horse became its owner, and the death penalty was mandatory."[6]

After the Indians, the next people to come into the territory were the Spanish. Then the French took a fancy to the area and ruled for a short time until Mexico conquered it. Finally, Anglos from the United States settled the vast plains of Texas, eventually forming the independent Republic of Texas.

In 1836 the Republic of Texas based its law on an interesting blend of the Spanish civil code, the code of Napoleon of Louisiana, and English common law. In 1840 Texas officially adopted English common law and repealed all Mexican laws prior to September 1, 1836, except those concerning land grants, colonization, and mineral rights.[7]

In 1845 Texas joined the United States, claiming territory extending into present-day Wyoming. In 1850 the state's present boundaries were set, and military rule came into the Trans-Pecos. The government built forts to protect travelers who wanted to cross the arid land to California and Oregon.[8]

During the Civil War, Federal troops evacuated and Confederate troops moved in for a short time. When the Confederates left, the Indians once again applied tomahawk justice in answer to prior abuses and threats of the white man.[9]

When the Federal troops returned after the Civil War, their first job was to clear out the Indians and the outlaws. For a time, tomahawk justice overlapped hang-and-shoot justice practiced by outlaws and vigilantes. Then came the land rush of the 1880s. Railroads arrived. Settlers claimed land. Ranchers, farmers, and sheepherders looked to the courts for justice.[10]

One answer to this plea for justice was the establishment in January 1917 of the 83rd Judicial District by the Texas legislature. Governor James E. Ferguson appointed James Cornell as first judge.[11]

The 83rd District is further than nearer to other districts from a geographical as well as a cultural viewpoint. Within its boundaries, long stretches of western landscapes make getting to court a long, difficult trek, and within the boundaries we find Spanish, Indian, and Anglo cultural influences.

Because of these factors, a unique western legal community developed. Attorneys represented their friends and neighbors rather than strangers. This was true in the 1970s when Ernest Williams, a witness, drawled to the attorney questioning him in court, "Look, son, you need to know how to ask the right questions." Three-fourths of the people in the courtroom silently agreed as they patiently educated another lawyer.[12]

Two of the main problems for the western courts were getting enough qualified jurors and finding times to hold court sessions. Finding acceptable jurors was complicated by the citizens' reluctance to serve and by lawyers' firm convictions about juror qualifications. In 1878 Bernardo Torres was excused from serving on a Pecos County jury in Fort Stockton because of an unusual excuse--Indian depredations on his ranch.[13] More recently, some high-school graduates, when summoned for jury duty, claimed they did not understand English.

Lack of qualified jurors also resulted from the attorneys' knowledge that citizens raised outside the area may not understand the West Texas mind into which, for instance, the right of self-defense is deeply ingrained. A potential juror was pronounced unacceptable to serve on the jury because he came from east of the Mississippi, where, the defense lawyer said, self-defense was not acceptable.[14]

In the 83rd everyone understood that court sessions were never held (1) during cattle shipping time and (2) during deer season when ranchers are paid from $150 to $1,500 per hunter.

Cattle shipping time is a busy one for the community with the round-up of cattle, transporting them to holding pens, loading them on truck or train, and shipping them to distribution centers.

Deer season in the fall is equally busy with hunters from across the United States and further away arriving for stays on the ranch which can extend to several weeks. Ranchers' wives are busy preparing enough food and entertaining. Men are busy taking the hunters out over the ranches, looking for deer to kill. Then carcasses must be cleaned and stored or butchered and, many times, taxidermists must be contacted to take charge of prize heads. Game wardens cover as much territory as they can to be sure no illegal deer are taken, and all are watching for poachers. Who has time to serve on a jury?

Of course, the excuse works the other way also. One November evening during deer season Federal Judge Lucius Bunton telephoned Judge Bill Earney, state district judge of the 83rd.

"Tell Judge Bunton," Judge Earney's wife said to the long-distance operator, "that Judge Earney is in an important meeting and will call him in a day or two when he returns from Austin."

"Tell Judge Earney," Judge Bunton intoned in a deep voice, "to call me as soon as he bags his white tail deer."[15]

In addition to juror selection and session timing, witnesses also represented the special character of the district. The only witness to an alleged horse stealing was on the stand and, when asked to tell about the incident, replied that he had heard of no incident.

"Well, what are we doing in court then?" the disconcerted lawyer asked.[16]

In another case, Jimmy Mills, Marfa plumber, changed his statement about the actions of the accused man. The district attorney was now in deep trouble.

"Mr. Mills," he said almost in tears, "that is not what you told me the other day!"

"Oh, I was just talking then, but now I'm swearin'."[17]

Truthfulness is a part of the West and is instilled in the young people at an early age.

Fritz Kahl, mayor of Marfa in 1997, recalled a court case involving Dr. and Mrs. Donald McIvor, the owners of the U Up U Down Ranch, northwest of Fort Davis up Limpia Canyon.

"A welder at the ranch," Mayor Kahl remembered, "found an old pear burner tossed out on a trash heap and asked if he could have it. Earl Grubb, working on the ranch, and his young son, Gibby, were there." Earl said the man could have it but warned that it was a dangerous piece of equipment.

"The man tried to light it. There was a residue of gas in the burner, and it exploded, shattering the welder's arm," Kahl continued.

"While Earl tried to stem the bleeding of the man's arm, he sent Gibby racing to the ranch house where Dr. McIvor was." They took the welder to the Brewster County Hospital in Alpine. When Dr. McIvor arrived, he "literally pushed Dr. Malone Hill aside and began working on the man, putting his arm back together again. Later the man sued the McIvors for personal injury," Kahl said.

"Because the McIvors' residence was in New Hampshire, the case was tried in Pecos in federal district court with Judge R. E. Thomason presiding. Gibby Grubb, about eleven years old and slicked up within an inch of his life--bow tie and all, was to be a witness," Kahl added.

"Just a minute," the judge said. Getting off the bench, he walked around to Gibby and asked directly,

"Son, do you know the importance of being a witness?"

The big-eyed, earnest little boy answered solemnly, "Yes, sir."

"Do you know what telling the truth is?"

"Yes, sir."

"What is it?"

"My daddy said he would beat me half to death if I didn't tell the truth."

Judge Thomason straightened up. "Bailiff, swear in the witness."

"Later one of the attorneys told me Gibby's testimony was the key to the case and the McIvors won the case," Kahl finished.[18]

To begin this rich, West Texas tradition, the first judge of the 83rd took the law into his own hands on the streets of Del Rio late one June evening in 1921.

James Cornell

Courtesy of Houston Metropolitan Research Center, Houston Public Library and with the cooperation of Ester Sanchez and Natalie Mellard, Marfa Public Library, Marfa, Texas

Chapter 2

The First Judge—James Cornell

He was six-feet-one-inch tall with a fair complexion. Known as a personable man, he got along easily with people, that is, with the exception of one man. They had been friends since childhood in the ranch country around Bracketville and Sonora in the 1880s.[1]

James Cornell passed the Texas State Bar examination in 1896, practiced law in Marfa for two years, was appointed assistant county attorney for Bexar County in 1898, and in 1901 began private law practice. In 1917, appointed by Governor James E. Ferguson, he became the first judge of the newly created 83rd Judicial District.[2]

Although the frontier was gradually fading into civilization, the territory's size created its own set of difficulties and, sometimes, Cornell came late to court. On May 12, 1918, after waiting three days for the judge to appear in Fort Stockton, the three attorneys elected one of their group, W. A. Hadden, to act as judge pro tem. Hadden heard several cases before dismissing witnesses and jurors to return on May 29, 1918.[3]

The *Fort Stockton Pioneer* observed that jurors and witnesses had been "a little provoked" with Cornell.[4] W. T. O. Holman, a prominent Val Verde County rancher who lived in Del Rio, was more than a little provoked with his friend, Cornell. Trouble had been brewing between the two men for a long time.

Their story begins around 1901. Holman had been tried and acquitted of the murder of Tom Carson in Kerrville. Cornell had participated in the trial as a witness against Holman. The *San Angelo Daily Standard* reported on November 18, 1921, that a land deal of 1908 caused the first break in the lifelong friendship. Several years before 1921, a local option election had been held in Sutton County with the two men on opposite sides. Then in December 1920, according to the paper, there was a meeting of the two men and Holman said, "Jim Cornell, if you brought me here to quarrel, I'll kill you" and reached for a gun. The Christmas Eve crowd yelled, "Don't do it!" and Holman put his gun away.

According to the newspaper, a Captain W. W. Davis of El Paso, former Texas Ranger, said Holman told him, "Every time Cornell comes down here (Del Rio), he gets drunk and it would be the easiest thing in the world to bump him off." According to Davis, Holman offered Davis $5,000 to have Cornell killed.

Cornell heard of the threat and felt justified in carrying a pistol with him when he went to Del Rio to attend the annual Sheep and Goat Raisers Association meeting. As a member of the executive committee, he was scheduled to respond to the welcoming speech. After he checked into the Saint Charles Hotel, he went to the nearby Central Pharmacy with Albert Sargent, his nephew.

In the meantime, Holman, who had attended a baseball game with his nine-year-old grandson, Holman Day, brought his grandson to the door of the pharmacy while Cornell was inside.

Sargent, seeing Holman, warned his uncle in a loud voice, "Look out, Uncle Jim!"

Although many witnesses told significantly different stories, the fact is that Cornell fired. Holman fell to the sidewalk. Cornell continued to fire. After five shots, Cornell leaned over and pulled Holman's pistol from an underarm holster. Apparently, Holman had reached for it, but it caught on his shirt.

Holman Day told another story and said his grandfather was holding him by the hand so he would not have been reaching for his gun. E. E. Rhodes testified he saw Cornell grab Holman by the shoulder and whirl him around.

Nevertheless, Holman was dead, and Cornell went back to his hotel room where Walter Gillis, Cliff C. Belcher, and George W. Thurmond, all lawyers, joined him. Cornell knew he needed to get out of town in a hurry because Holman had four grown sons, one nicknamed "Big," and the boys were looking for revenge while their friends tried to stop them. Cornell surrendered to the Texas Rangers, who hurried him to Bracketville.

The Sheep and Goat Raisers Association held its meeting, as scheduled, the morning after the shooting. Bob Martin, president, complained that everyone was talking about the shooting instead of the low prices of wool and cheap mutton. As it turned out, he was also the foreman of the grand jury that indicted Cornell for murder that Friday.

Cornell maintained he was indicted at his own request. Trial was set for October but was postponed until November 14, 1921, in Val Verde County. All this time Cornell continued to hold court in his district.

After a five-day trial, the jury found him not guilty, and he continued as judge. Despite that fact, the Marfa newspaper, *The New Era*, reported on December 24, 1921, that he had resigned. The judge immediately wired Marfa with facts to the contrary; however, Cornell was in trouble.

The *Alpine Avalanche* reported on February 16, 1922, that Judge Joseph Jones was holding court in Alpine for Cornell. The editor continued in a testy manner, writing that Judge Cornell had been in Alpine "a few days before" and had granted a change of venue from Brewster County to Presidio County in a case "for what reason is a mystery to many. The act of the court has been the object of much comment."

Cornell chose not to run for office in the 1922 election. C. R. Sutton of Marfa was elected and convened court in January 1923.[5]

There were many unanswered questions about the Holman shooting. Mrs. J. E. White Sr., called "Mamacita" by her friends and neighbors in the Trans-Pecos, had been a young wife in Del Rio at that time.

In 1983 she was a tiny, gray-haired southern lady. I called her one day to ask her about the incident.

"Mamacita, you knew the Cornell family of Sonora, didn't you?" I began.

"Oh, yes. They were such lovely people," she answered.

"You knew the Holmans, didn't you?"

"They were fine, lovely people too," she answered.

"Tell me, just what was the trouble between the two men?"

She gave a delicate pause, then said, "My dear, I don't remember a thing."[6]

Some questions will forever remain unanswered. Those who knew the answers have since gone to their graves with their secrets, and those who are still among the living choose to keep their counsel.

The first judge of the 83rd Judicial District was of the true Western mold, believing in the right of self-defense. Some people were not happy with him, but as one judge said, "Judges always make half the people unhappy with their decisions."[7]

When the next judge, C. R. Sutton, took office, he definitely made some people very unhappy--by sentencing a man to death by hanging.

C. R. Sutton, circa 1942
*Courtesy of Sarabelle S. Sutton, daughter-in-law of
Judge and Mrs. Sutton, Uvalde, Texas*

Chapter 3

The Judges' Judge –C. R. Sutton

As an elected official, a state judge must have the favorable opinion of the majority of the electorate in his district. C. R. Sutton held that majority for eighteen years, from January 1923 until December 1940. When he resigned to run for another office, some of his friends voted against him because they wanted him to remain as state judge.[1]

"You knew he was a judge when you saw him," James Weatherby of Big Lake remembered. "He was a good and fair judge, and he acted like one."[2]

Many definitions and lists have been written about the characteristics of a good judge. The ultimate definition was written in a 1985 letter: "He is a good judge. He ruled in favor of the people I am interested in."[3]

Born on a farm in Llano County on December 27, 1886, C. R. Sutton attended local schools and went to college at San Marcos--the school with the old, red-brick building with the spires on the north side of town, Southwest Texas State University.

He attended the University of Texas Law School and left that institution as soon as he learned he had passed the bar exam. The reason was simple. He said, "I was out of money."

In 1913 he moved to Marfa, served in the army during World War I, returned to Marfa to practice law, and married Willie Colbert Mimms, daughter of a pioneer Marfa rancher. They had four sons.[4]

When Sutton took office in 1923, he was handed one of the most difficult tasks a judge faces-- sentencing a man to death by hanging.

Harvey Hughes was hungry, and fellow hobo-- young Clifford Rogers--bought supper for him in Marathon, paying with a twenty dollar bill and pocketing the change. Rogers had left his bride of three weeks in Philadelphia to go to California, where a job waited for him. When he got settled, the new Mrs. Rogers would join him. No one understood why he chose to ride the rails.

At Marathon, Hughes and Rogers hopped a freight train going west. Somewhere between Marathon and Alpine, Hughes beat and shot Rogers, taking his watch and other small items including the change from the twenty dollars. When the train pulled into Alpine, Rogers called for help and the trainmen found him lying in the corner of a boxcar.

"It's hell to feed a man and have him shoot you in the back," Rogers said as he lay dying.

Hughes escaped but was soon captured at Toronto, a section house on the railroad five miles west of

Alpine. At his first trial, Hughes was found guilty and sentenced to death by hanging. The appeals process delayed final sentencing until Sutton's term of office.

In October 1922 Hughes took matters into his own hands when Sheriff E. E. Townsend of Alpine, his deputy, and several Alpine men were in San Antonio at federal court. He jimmied the lock to his cell, and when the deputy's wife came at 8 p.m. to check on the prisoners, he jumped her and escaped although she said she "grappled" with him.

An ice-cold rain fell that October night, and the quickly gathered posse had trouble finding the trail. A description of the escapee was sent out over the telegraph: "About twenty years old, medium weight and height, blue eyes and light brown hair."

A week later, he was found asleep in a house at the same railroad section where he had originally been captured. He had been out in the rain and cold for several days, and he did not resist. There was a second trial. Hughes pled insanity, but on March 1, 1923, the Alpine jury found him sane. In Sutton's third month as judge, he passed the sentence of death by hanging and set the date of execution for April 7, 1923.

Some of the local citizens circulated a petition asking for a stay of execution, but it took place as scheduled. On Saturday, April 7, 1923, behind a high fence on the north side of the courthouse, Hughes was executed. Only a few witnesses were present including three sheriffs of the area and the Reverend J. A. McMillan of the Alpine Christian Church, who offered a prayer.

The trap was sprung during the prayer so Hughes would not know. The men at the execution were compassionate, not vindictive, but the sentence had to be carried out. Hughes went to his death calmly.

In a letter published posthumously by the *Alpine Avalanche*, Hughes said he became a habitual criminal, learning tricks of the trade in a boys' industrial school in Ohio, where he was sent when he was eleven. He claimed he had found God and had been baptized. A funeral service was held for him at the Alpine Christian Church, and he was buried in the Alpine cemetery.[5]

Meanwhile, at the other end of the district in Reagan County, things were getting ready to pop. It had all started in May 1923 with "She's a blowin' in!"

Texas tea gushed from the earth, and surrounding towns boomed. It was a hard-working, get-rich-quick, brawling time, and local authorities discreetly overlooked Prohibition laws.[6]

The good citizens of Reagan County worried, and by October 17, 1925, they were looking for a cleaner, more law-abiding community. In desperation they circumvented local officials and took their complaints to Sheriff D. S. Barker and District Attorney Joe G. Montague, both of Pecos County.

As a result of their pleas, lawmen from several surrounding counties quietly drifted into the towns of Big Lake and Best. Among them were three county sheriffs, one ex-sheriff, two deputy sheriffs, one special investigator, three U. S. Customs agents, three Prohibition agents, and one district attorney.

When the female proprietor of a watering place in Best cordially invited two men to come back, the men obliged on the next night with warrant in hand. That Saturday night was a busy one.

Raids that Saturday night garnered quite a treasure for law enforcement officials. Authorities captured 2,251 quarts of illicit beverages, 546 gallons of corn whiskey, 7 bottles of tequila, 5 bottles of Cognac, a wholesale liquor house, 12 retail houses, 1 still located one-and-a-half miles southwest of Best, and a brewery, one-and-a-half miles northeast of Best. In addition, sixteen people were arrested. The whiskey and other edibles were taken to the Pecos County jail for safekeeping, and the still and brewery were destroyed.

Suddenly judicial business picked up. Reagan County had poked along for years with a few criminal cases here and there. According to the San Angelo newspaper, from between 40 and 50 cases over several years, the number jumped to a total of 147 criminal indictments over the next few days.

When Judge Sutton impaneled the grand jury, he cautioned it to "clean up" Reagan County and warned law enforcement officers that if it were not cleaned up, "measures to bring about improved conditions would be devised and placed in effect."

The busy grand jury turned in thirty-four indictments that day, twenty-eight of them for Prohibition violations. There were so many indictments that W. E. McDermott, clerk of the court in Big Lake, sent a request to Jesse T. Couch, clerk of the court of Tom Green County, asking for two hundred blank indictments.

In the report to the court, one of the officers stated that, at the Best Social Club, it was necessary to join the club for one dollar before buying drinks. One officer proudly displayed the membership card he purchased the night of the raids. He said that he and a fellow officer went into a little room in the northeast corner of the building and bought two glasses of whiskey at fifty cents apiece and drank the beverage. He said, "It was intoxicating."

The officers told of another house that had three rooms which operated in three different ways. In the front room, patrons could buy soda pop. In the second room, whiskey was sold. Finally, in the third room, customers passed their time gambling at poker and other games while still others were kibitzing.

At the same time, many "booze sellers" were pleading guilty in federal court in San Angelo. Judge Edward A. Meek obliged by setting up an assembly line in the courtroom.

He received a plea of not guilty and told the jury it was their "perfunctory" duty to render a verdict and find the defendants guilty. Walter Pitt of Coleman, seated nearby, signed the verdict and handed it to Jesse Couch, clerk.

Sentences varied from $5 to $750 and three months in jail. One owner of a "soft drink stand" received a large fine for selling intoxicating beverages while his helper, a "soda jerker," went free. Husbands received harsher sentences than their wives, who were usually excused at the request of their husbands.

Back in Big Lake, the court sessions were being held in the Crystal Theater, the town's movie theater.

Reagan County had recently voted to change the county seat from Stiles, where there was a courthouse and jail, to Big Lake, where there were more people but no facilities. Prisoners who could not make bail were held overnight in Best, Stiles, and Fort Stockton jails. During the day, prisoners were held under guard at the Big Lake Hotel.

In addition to prisoners, there were three Texas Rangers and seven other officers as guards. Add to these the families of the prisoners, the lawyers, newspaper reporters, and court officials, and the theater had a full house with standing room only.

Sutton heard one murder trial, but after the jury had deliberated for thirty hours without a consensus, the judge dismissed them and declared a mistrial. He set up a special session for December to act on 141 liquor cases and parceled out the cases over the district, a few in different counties, to lighten the load.

He started another murder trial, but after exhausting all qualified prospective jurors in the county, he moved the trial to Presidio County. The trial finally began on August 1, 1928, ending with the defendant receiving a five-year suspended sentence.

After that murder trial, the jurors as well as Sutton were exhausted. To relax, he spent the weekend with his brother, John F. Sutton, also a district judge, in San Angelo. After several raucous days in Big Lake, the judge drove back to Marfa through the long, lonely 190 miles, savoring the blessed quiet.[7]

On March 9, 1928, the civil docket in Fort Stockton was the heaviest in the history of the court with 180 suits filed and with more attorneys in town than had ever been seen before. More than $20 million in oil and land was involved. At stake was the "much litigated Yates and Smith oil field territory," the so-called "vacancy strip," one of the richest oil-producing lands in the state of Texas.

In 1924 Mrs. M. A. Smith had sold oil and gas leases to representatives of Gulf Production Company. However, her family maintained that she had not been competent to make such decisions. On June 8, 1928, a jury said her actions were not binding, and millions of dollars began to change hands--among them, those belonging to W. H. Colquitt as receiver for the Smith Estate.[8] As much interest as the land cases caused, murder trials were responsible for far more emotion and upheaval in the towns.

In August 1934 Texas Ranger W. F. Hale Jr. and J. S. Weatherby, a rancher from the rugged Pinto Canyon of southern Presidio County, were indicted for the murder of Pablo Prieto, a rancher neighbor of Weatherby's. Hale, Weatherby, and a Ranger Curie were also indicted for assault and attempted murder of Gregorio Prieto, Pablo's brother.

Mrs. Gregorio Prieto, sister-in-law of the dead man, testified that the Rangers came to her house to investigate a shooting on June 4, 1934, when a bullet had gone through Weatherby's truck. He claimed he and one of his sons were in the truck at the time.

Mrs. Prieto said that her husband, Gregorio, told the Rangers he knew nothing about the shooting and then asked them to leave and return some other time. As Gregorio approached the door, one of the Rangers shot him. The Rangers left, but returned the next day,

June 5, 1934, and broke down the door when the family refused to open it. Gregorio was lying on the floor with Pablo sitting beside him. The Rangers shot and killed Pablo and shot Gregorio fifteen times.

However, Ranger Hale testified he went to the Prieto house to investigate the shooting of Weatherby's truck, and Gregorio came to the door with a gun. Someone in Hale's group fired; the group left, returned later, and broke down the door. Pablo was sitting on the floor with a gun in his hand. Hale said he shot in self-defense.

Several area ranchers testified that the Weatherbys ran sheep and goats, and some of the livestock were missing. The Weatherbys blamed the Prietos. In contrast, many local citizens said the Prietos were good people and would not take what was not theirs.

When the jury found Hale not guilty, he immediately left the crowded courtroom and joined his wife, who was waiting in their car, packed and ready to leave town. Feelings were intense, and Hale knew he had better leave the area. The marks of the shooting ran deep. The Prietos sold out and left Presidio County as did the Weatherbys.

The *Big Bend Sentinel* of Marfa carried the story of the trial and the verdict. The story ended with the somber statement, "Probably for the first and only time in the history of trials of any kind in this or any state, the accused, Ranger Hale, carried firearms in the courtroom. Ranger Hale was not deprived of his gun but wore it during the hearing of the witnesses."

People in the courtroom saw Hale shift in his seat to expose the gun to the witnesses as they testified.[9]

Another murder trial began in the Presidio County Courthouse in January 1939. A soldier stationed at Fort D. A. Russell, Charles Shindler, was accused of murder in a case that foreshadowed Perry Mason because Shindler was acquitted on the fine point of a dirty shirt. One witness said the accused wore a dirty, torn shirt. A corporal testified that he had removed Shindler's shirt and it was neither torn nor dirty.

During the impaneling of the jury, Shindler's attorney challenged one of the prospective jurors.

The accused jerked the lawyer's coat and whispered, "Take him! Take him!"

The angry attorney complied, sat down, and demanded of his client, "Why?"

"I play poker with him every Saturday night," the defendant said.

"That could be either good or bad," the lawyer gloomily predicted.

Shindler was subsequently acquitted. He was shipped to the Italian war zone during World War II. Toward the end of the war, Shindler returned to visit Marfa, his chest covered with medals, decorations, and awards for valor. He had been a commando in Italy. While talking to a friend one day, he touched the ribbons thoughtfully and said, "You know, the government gave me these for doing what the state wanted to send me to the chair for."[10]

In December 1937 Judge Sutton made a speech which probably gave him indigestion three years later. He described the system of the state's courts to the Uvalde Rotary Club. He stated that the jury system was a fair and equitable one and that people should look forward to performing their public duty. He castigated those who did not want to serve. Then the denoucment: "The eleven appeals courts in Texas are not needed, and I hope the voters will one day abolish all eleven of them."[11]

On February 2, 1940, C. R. Sutton announced for the office of associate justice of the Court of Civil Appeals, Eighth District, El Paso--one of the courts he had previously wished to abolish. The West Texas judicial community had a way of reminding him of his words.[12] However, C. R. Sutton was politically astute and was elected in November after a run-off election in August. He assumed his duties in January of 1941.[13]

The eighteen years of Judge Sutton's tenure saw a gradual change in the Trans-Pecos country. The excitement of building a new country flowed into the excitement of the oil strikes. The Depression years were difficult, but they were easier in the rural Trans-Pecos than in the cities.

The courts saw many murder trials among the cases for clearing land titles, leases, and oil royalties as well as a few divorces. In the mid-1930s, business began a slow recovery as the sounds of war grew nearer. Draft notices arrived in the mail. Fort D. A. Russell at Marfa reopened, now with chemical warfare companies in place of the old cavalry units.

Judge Sutton moved on to the appeals court in El Paso, and H. O. Metcalfe of Marfa was appointed by Governor W. Lee O'Daniel to take Sutton's place.[14] Among Metcalfe's cases was the particular case of the juror's pregnant wife, a case for which he will be remembered in law journals.

**Hunter Orgain Metcalfe,
circa 1950**

Chapter 4

Old-Time Judge—H. O. Metcalfe

He did not say "the law," but "THE LAW" with a respectful deference, and there was nothing he liked better than a hard-fought court case, using his well-trained voice on the jury to its best effect.

Hunter Orgain Metcalfe was born in Hutto, Texas, in 1887 and worked his way through Southwestern University at Georgetown, Texas, waiting tables. After graduation in 1909, he taught chemistry and coached football at Orange High School with Professor J. E. Buckley although he said he knew less about football than he knew about the sciences.

Moving back to Georgetown, he became a secretary in the law office of D. W. Wilcox and Judge Harry N. Graves, where he read the law. He passed the bar exam, married, and opened his own law office on the courthouse square in Georgetown.

"Thank goodness, Uncle Reader (Mood) had a grocery store," attorney Metcalfe's wife recalled, "or we would have starved those first few months."

America entered World War I, and Metcalfe tried to enlist, but the recruiter refused his offer, saying, "No thanks. You have tuberculosis and have only three months to live."

In 1917 the cure for tuberculosis was bed rest. Metcalfe closed his office and, taking his wife and two-year-old daughter, moved in with his parents in San Antonio. After several months of complete rest, to everyone's surprise, he recovered. Then his doctor handed him another usual prescription for lung trouble at the time: "Go west."

Metcalfe did as his doctor ordered and moved to Marfa, where he found a job as a secretary with attorney C. E. Mead. After six months Mead said, "Hunter, you're no secretary."

Metcalfe's heart sank into his shoes.

"But," Mead continued to the delight of the young man, "you *are* a lawyer."

Thus the firm of Mead and Metcalfe was formed. In later years two state district judges and one federal judge came out of that small office.[1]

Governor W. Lee O'Daniel appointed Metcalfe to take Judge Sutton's place in January 1941. In 1942 and 1946 Metcalfe ran for the office unopposed.[2]

In his first year of office, he heard the case of the juror's pregnant wife, which caused Marfa people to chuckle. In August 1941 a Presidio man was indicted for assault with intent to murder. The jury panel gathered in the Marfa courthouse, and the judge listened to prospective jurors give reasons to be excused from jury duty. From experience, judges know that jurors can dream up some far-out excuses, but "my wife is expecting her baby any time now" is a valid excuse.

In August 1941 among the group of prospective jurors was Fox Parker Jr. Everyone in Marfa knew that Fox's wife, Alice, would soon produce their first child, and the cafe coffee crowd was making bets on the time. At that time jurors were sequestered and kept together day and night during a criminal trial. Fox had not asked to be excused, and the judge wondered why.

"Are there any others who need to be excused from jury duty?" Judge Metcalfe asked again.

Fox sat silently.

"Mr. Parker, do you have any reason to be excused from jury duty?" the judge asked.

"No, your honor."

Well, the judge thought, a man ought to know when his own child will be born. He continued the jury procedure and Fox was chosen as one of the twelve to serve. Three days into the trial with the case going to the jury the next morning, a terrified bachelor neighbor of the Parkers scratched on a window screen of the judge's house at three in the morning.

"For God's sake, get the judge! I just took Alice to the hospital!" the neighbor shouted.

Muttering things about costing the county money and people time, Metcalfe, to his wife's dismay, donned his old, brown, Sears bathrobe over his pajamas, his beat-up bedroom slippers, and his old fishing hat and stalked across the dark street, across the courthouse lawn, and into El Paisano Hotel, where the jury was being kept overnight.

"Get me Sheriff Joe Bunton, the DA, and all the lawyers in this case and have them meet me in the lobby," he ordered the startled night clerk.

One by one the men arrived to meet the judge in the darkened lobby and, at four in the morning, they held a conference.

Metcalfe was ready to explode. "Nick just took Alice to the hospital, and I'm not about to keep a man from his wife at a time like this. Get Fox up. I'll declare a mistrial."

Sheriff Bunton was a big, easy-going man. "Now, Hunter, I don't think you really want to do this," he soothed. "I think I have a solution." He explained his idea to the judge, who gave his permission to the unusual plan.

Sheriff Bunton escorted all twelve jurors to the delivery room of the hospital. Alice, surrounded by her doctor and nurses, gave birth. Fox stood a few feet from his wife, pale but determined not to pass out. For his part, Sheriff Bunton stood at the swinging doors between the delivery room and the waiting room. During the whole process, he watched Fox to his left, and to his right, the other members of the jury. The sheriff kept all twelve jurors within his view in the waiting room--all of whom displayed different states of agitation, depending on whether they were fathers or not.

For her part, Alice worked hard and produced six-pound, seven-ounce Lilbrum Lewis Fox Parker III at 7:30 a.m. on August 15, 1941, an anniversary present for her husband. After the blessed event, a shaken jury returned to the courtroom, seemingly not softened by their experience, and returned a verdict of guilty with five years to serve in the penitentiary. The defense appealed the case on the grounds that the jury was not kept together. The appeal was denied, but the case was reversed later on another point of law.

In fiction, the events of two years later might sound contrived, but sometimes fact is stranger than fiction. Two years later, almost to the day, another criminal trial began in Presidio County. Alice Parker was expecting--again. Fox was called for jury duty--again. He entered the courtroom laughing.

The judge, seeing Fox, grabbed the gavel, banged it, and roared, "Sheriff, get that man out of here, and if he returns, I'll hold him in contempt of court!"

The trial proceeded without Fox Parker Jr., and on August 13, 1943, Elizabeth Parker was born.[3]

Two other events during Metcalfe's term of office caused as much furor at the Pecos County Courthouse in Fort Stockton as the Parker episode. In September 1941 S. C. Hustead, a sixty-eight-year-old filling station operator from Grandfalls, confessed to the murder of R. M. Reed at Reed's ranch house near Fort Stockton. Officers were led to the accused by matching pieces of broken glass at a wrecked gate with glass from a car's broken headlight found in a local wrecking yard.

Hustead was arrested on a Saturday and gave a statement to a stenographer on Monday while in the presence of several witnesses: Sheriff Dan B. Bihl; Texas Rangers Leo Bishop and Pat Talliaferro of

Alpine; Game Warden Ray Willoughby of Alpine; Maurice Bullock, Pecos County attorney; and Alan R. Fraser, district attorney. They witnessed his confession in the grand jury room on the third floor of the courthouse.

Hustead signed the confession and said he was resigned to his fate. Turning quickly, he jumped head first from the open third-story window, landing on the concrete floor of the open porch twenty-five feet below.[4] Hustead, realizing his crime would necessarily bring the death penalty, ended his life quickly. The next shocker had a much happier ending.

In October 1946, during a trial for burglary, the accused realized things were not going well for him. He whipped out a bottle, gulped its contents, and asked the officers to tell his wife and baby good-bye. However, to his surprise, the liquid was not poisonous as the defendant believed. Instead of delivering him into the arms of death, it gave the accused a good, twelve-hour sleep.[5]

When court was held in Marfa during Metcalfe's term, an interesting custom developed after a trial ended. Attorneys and court officials, friends and neighbors all, walked across the street from the courthouse to the Metcalfe home for some socializing.

While the judge barbecued cabrito, the guests visited and taste-tested the meat. The aroma of the barbecued goat--mingled with that of frijoles, chile verde, southern cornbread, and fresh coffee--filled the neighborhood. Tossed salad, real butter for the hot bread, and crisp, sweet icebox cookies always accompanied the meal. In good weather the court adversaries, and in many cases lifelong friends, enjoyed the feast together in the backyard.

The only uneasy lawyer among the guests would be the newest, who sat and stared in amazement at the men who a short time before were tearing each other apart in the courtroom. Here they sat, laughed, talked, exchanged jokes, and made plans to go fishing together.

The evening broke up about nine o'clock when someone noticed the time and said, "We'd better leave. It's the judge's bedtime, and he'll be going to bed before we leave." And he would have too.

On December 5, 1947, Metcalfe announced his resignation effective January 1, 1948, and Governor Beauford Jester appointed Alan R. Fraser to take his place.[6]

At the beginning of the Metcalfe term, men were being drafted and leaving for military service, the Marfa Army Airfield opened, the troops at Fort D. A. Russell increased, and the Trans-Pecos watched the Rio Grande border for enemy activities. Pearl Harbor accelerated the call of West Texas men. Soon death notices of servicemen were front page news, making these difficult years.

There were fewer murder trials, but in 1945 as news stories of servicemen returning home increased, so did the number of divorces. Felonies increased as the postwar adjustment period began. Alan R. Fraser, former district attorney, came home from Europe and brought his European court knowledge with him to use in the 83rd as judge.

Alan R. Fraser

Courtesy of Archives of the Big Bend, Bryan Wildenthal Library,
Sul Ross State University, Alpine, Texas

Chapter 5

World War II Veteran—Alan R. Fraser

Alan Fraser, the future judge of the 83rd, poked his head out of the basement. He stared across the rubble left from bombs and battles and listened. He heard troops marching. Certain they were American or Allied troops, he and his companion scrambled from their hiding place and ran forward. A glimpse of German helmets made them do a rapid about-face to "beat a hasty retreat to the dungeon."

Hunkered down, they hoped to escape discovery and decided to eat their rations, "refusing to die on an empty stomach, adding insult to injury."[1]

Fraser soon rejoined his unit and wrote the home folks in Alpine and Marfa. "Thanks for the cigars. . . . Things go on here. Mighty bloody and be prepared for shocks and bad news as this is a tough fight. We are fine but miss things like a glass of milk, an egg, a steak, Mex [sic] food, real bread, coffee, pie, ice cream, milk shakes, our friends, lcisure, comfort, warmth, Texas sunshine, but here we are alive and well and we'll be home someday."2

Alan Fraser was a transplanted Yankee. Born in Rixford, Pennsylvania, he received his formal education from Washington University, the University of Buffalo, and the University of Texas at Austin and began law practice in Austin in 1932. He moved to Alpine in 1933.

His political career took the usual route of city attorney to district attorney, but in 1943 he resigned to go into the army. That army service did not follow the usual route. He was assigned to the British army for a short time, and while in England and Scotland, conducted a series of lectures at St. Andrews University on "Crime Prevention through Education," a pet topic he had emphasized back home in West Texas.

He also addressed civic clubs, service groups, and welfare organizations on the same topic to keep him busy, plus worked with an international quiz program for which he was the master of ceremonies. In 1945 he went to Lillehammer, Norway, to prosecute German Captain Wolfgang Blell for the murder on May 13, 1945, of a Russian ex-POW just two days after V-E Day. When the military tribunal of American, British, and Norwegian officers handed down the death sentence, the citizens of Lillehammer were jubilant and heaped a mound of flowers on Fraser's desk. The Oslo newspaper *Morganposten* said of the trial, Fraser exhibited "justice, humanity, discretion, culture, and integrity." What an image to live up to! He subsequently became chief of the legal section of the military government in Frankfurt, Germany, where he was responsible for the city courts.[3]

He was back in Alpine, in the Texas sunshine, by September of 1947 and was appointed the new judge of the 83rd by Governor Beauford Jester, the appointment to be effective January 1, 1948.[4]

During his years as judge, several superlatives occurred. On January 30, 1948, because of the coldest recorded temperature to date, he dismissed the petit jury in Marfa. The temperature got so low, the big, old Presidio County courtroom with its high ceilings could not be heated by the coal-burning, pot-bellied stove.[5]

The shortest term of court in the district happened in Fort Stockton on September 3, 1948, when Fraser held court with only two brief civil cases and eighteen criminal cases on the docket. Many of the accused criminals had not been arrested.[6]

The biggest and the costliest trial up to that time was the Babb murder trial. It had all the elements of an intense comic-drama--a running gunfight in the primitive southern Brewster County ranch country at Lajitas along the Rio Grande, threats and counter-threats to kill, shenanigans among the lawyers, and two jurors smuggling whiskey.[7]

After the trial in Marfa, one attorney wrote, "I . . . had lots of fun."[8]

The background of this trial began in December 1946. The United States government closed the Mexican border because of an outbreak of foot-and-mouth disease among Mexican cattle. The highly contagious disease can lead to many complications in cloven-footed animals. The only known treatment at that time was to slaughter the infected animals and burn or bury the carcasses. The land then had to be left without livestock for several months. Vaccinations and quarantines could control the disease but not eradicate it.[9]

In order to keep infected livestock, mainly cattle, from straying across the Rio Grande from Mexico, men called "river riders" were hired by the federal government to patrol along the river. Stanley Jeffers, age thirty-one, was hired to watch the land around Lajitas and lived in a rent-free house, courtesy of W. L. Babb.

Babb, age thirty-three, was foreman of the Lewis Llewenthal ranch and supervisor of the Llewenthal wax plant, which processed the candelilla weed for wax to be used commercially. The weed grew wild throughout the ranch country and in Mexico, and many people brought sacks of it to Babb at Lajitas at the Llewenthal windmill, a landmark.

Both the Jeffers and Babb families knew the country well, having owned land and lived there for several years. They lived in houses within shooting distance of each other, yet despite their proximity, rumors of "bad blood" between them circulated throughout the sparsely settled country.

There had been arguments between the two men over the crossing of cattle at the river. Babb also accused Jeffers of receiving payoffs from Mexicans who were pulling the candelilla weed in Mexico and the Big Bend National Park, which was illegal, and bringing the partially processed plants to Jeffers. Since the two men lived not far from each other, according to open-country standards, the situation was sticky.

While witnesses gave conflicting testimonies at the trial, they all agreed upon the basic story. The night before the killing, the Jeffers family had been target shooting. Babb said he saw the Jeffers car with its lights shining across the Rio Grande. He said he thought they were firing into Mexico and that Mexicans were firing back, possibly with the idea of raiding the wax plant where Babb kept between $5,000 and $10,000 to pay people who brought wax to him.

Late in the afternoon the next day Babb sent his "little boy" Kent to water his horse. When bullets flew near the house, Mrs. Babb called to her son to come inside. Babb with his brother, Smokey, got into the Babb car and started toward the Jeffers house. Meanwhile the two Jeffers brothers, Stanley and Joe, with their guest, Eugene Lefevre, in the back seat, drove their car toward Babb-—no horseback riding to this western confrontation.

The two cars stopped. Babb got out and walked to the Jeffers vehicle. The Jeffers said Babb came up cursing and saying he was going to kill them. Babb testified he walked to the car and said, "What the hell do you mean by letting those boys shoot toward our house?"

Babb said his pistol, a .38 caliber Smith and Wesson, was in his holster. Joe Jeffers changed previous testimony and said Babb held the pistol down at his side.

Brian Montague, defense attorney, questioned Joe.

Question: "Did you see Stanley Jeffers shoot W. L. Babb?"

Answer: "No. He didn't fire until after he was dead."

Babb said Stanley fired first, Babb returned the fire, and Stanley was killed instantly with a bullet through his head. Joe and Lefevre fell out the other side of the car, Lefevre running behind the Jeffers house to get his own German Lugar out of his car. Joe leveled a shotgun across the front of the car and fired at Babb, who was racing down the ravine toward his own house, yelling at his brother, Smokey, to get out of there.

Babb had been shot once in each shoulder. Mrs. Babb said she saw a man standing on the mesa shooting at her husband as he staggered toward the house.

"Stray" Lee, another river rider who lived nearby, heard the shots and went to the Jeffers house. When he told Joe he was going to take Babb to the hospital in Alpine, he said Joe said he would kill anybody who came out of the Babb house.

Lee finally went for Justice of the Peace H. W. Patterson of Terlingua, who came to the Babbs, but they waited several hours after dark before driving the wounded man to Alpine for medical attention. The roads were rough, and it was at least a hundred-mile drive.

Babb was indicted by the Brewster County grand jury for murder with malice. The trial was delayed several times--once because Gene Lefevre's wife was to have a baby with a possible Cesarean section and another time because a prime witness could not be located.

The first trial began in August 1949 in Alpine, but some ten days into the trial, a juror became ill. He was an old-time settler from Marathon country and was unaccustomed to being shut up with eleven other men day and night. He was earnestly trying to follow the testimony but was puzzled over the two different versions of an event presented by the state's attorney and the defense attorney.

When he began saying, "I didn't do it!" the court realized he was ill. Two doctors certified that if he continued as juror, it would be injurious to his health. Judge Fraser had to declare a mistrial, the bane of all judges, attorneys, and court officials, not to mention taxpayers of the county who foot the bill for the trial. The judge reset the trial for Presidio County in January 1950.

The Alpine jurors were not happy. They had been kept at night in the courtroom sleeping on cots.

"We even had to make our own beds," Earl Lankford said with a chuckle. "We had trouble sleeping because we had to keep the big old windows open, and there were no screens on them. The mosquitoes had fun."

"There was only one rest room in the courthouse, and it didn't have a shower or a bathtub. After five days, the court finally rented a couple of rooms at the Holland Hotel, and we took turns getting cleaned up."

The defense attorney, Brian Montague of Del Rio, was not happy. He met the district attorney, Travers Crumpton, by chance in the lobby of a San Antonio hotel. Crumpton told him about the time and place of the new setting. Montague had cases set for trial in Eagle Pass at that time, had not been notified, and loudly discussed it with Crumpton, who answered in a few, also loud, well-chosen words.

However, the second trial did begin in Marfa at the end of January 1950, but the defense attorneys filed a flurry of protests, asking for a directed dismissal. Grounds chosen were that the new trial put Babb in double jeopardy, that neither Babb nor his attorney had been present when the trial was reset, that there were not enough men in Presidio County to get a second and fair jury, that the Presidio County Jury Commission which drew the names for the jury panel was illegally constituted because the three members all lived north of the railroad tracks in Marfa and did not give full representation to the county, and on and on.

Fraser firmly wrote "denied" at the bottom of the documents, and the defense attorneys as firmly wrote "excepted" as they laid the groundwork for the appeals process later. The second trial lasted seven days. With fringe activities increasing the interest of the observers, spectators packed the courtroom.

The first juror chosen was W. A. Allison, a rancher, and on Sunday, the entire jury went to the Allison Ranch, twenty-nine miles south of Marfa, to spend the day. Peace officers went with them and kept sharp eyes on the activities.

During the trial, as the testimony droned on, the judge got up, carried a bucket of coal across the courtroom, and poured it into a pot-bellied stove. After dusting off his hands, he returned to the bench. H. O.

Metcalfe, a defense attorney, got up then and went to the stove to warm himself.

"He did a thorough job of it. Starting with the palms of his hands, he presented every part of his body to the heat emanating from the stove. He ended up raising first one foot and the other close to the side of the stove, meanwhile, listening closely to court proceedings," wrote a fascinated reporter.

Babb maintained a poker face throughout the trial, smoking four packs of cigarettes a day and toying with two long lengths of wrapping twine on the defense table. He sternly cautioned his lawyer not to move the twine.

The Babb family (W. L.; his wife; and his father, Boyce C. Babb, a Langtry rancher) drove the twenty-six miles between Alpine and Marfa each day because Marfa facilities were full. The jury was staying at the Crews Hotel, and most other places were rented to a movie crew and actors in town to film the movie *Deadfall*.

Peace officers guarded the Babbs all day and on their trips back and forth to Alpine because of rumors that someone would try to kill them. After seven long days, the charge finally went to the jury, and it took them exactly ten minutes to return the verdict of "We, the jury, find the defendant not guilty." Babb remained stoic. Mrs. Babb smiled. The defense had emphasized the right of self-defense and the right to carry arms in self-defense.

It was learned later that two of the jurors who liked their afternoon drinks got awfully dry. As they left the hotel one morning for the courthouse, one slipped a porter a hefty tip. He got a bottle of Scotch and a bottle of bourbon, wrapped them in some old clothes, and stashed them at the top of the jurors' closet. Eagerly returning to the hotel, the two jurors searched the closet. Alas, the sheriff had been there ahead of them. They remained dry but never found out who the snitch was.[10]

The furor over the Babb case had barely settled down when the murder of the Presidio County sheriff shook the Trans-Pecos, and the largest manhunt in the Big Bend to that time commenced.

Sheriff Otis "Blackie" Morrow drove to Presidio after dark one Saturday night in March 1950 to confer with Deputy Mack Tarwater. He left Tarwater at his home and started the sixty-mile return trip to Marfa. About eleven miles out of Presidio he stopped and picked up a Mexican citizen standing beside the highway.

When he began to question the man about his citizenship papers, there was a scuffle. The man got the sheriff's gun and shot him twice, jumping out of the car and racing away through the dark. Morrow apparently got out of the car and hung for a while on a barbed wire fence before dragging himself back into the car. He turned around and headed back for Presidio, but died within a mile.

Four young men from Marfa--W. A. Oatman, Jim Plumbley, Otis Devolin, and Bill Wheeles--were on their way home when they saw the car lights on the left side of the road and stopped to investigate. They found the sheriff's car crashed into a ditch and Morrow hanging halfway out the window. They hurried back to

Presidio and called Ernest Barnett, Marfa's deputy sheriff.

Outraged over a fellow officer's death, Trans-Pecos lawmen descended on Marfa ready to join in the search. About forty people--sheriffs, deputy sheriffs, Border Patrol men, Immigration men, FBI agents, city policemen, El Paso officers--all wanted to join the mounted posse. Police set up two-way, short-wave radio communications and put mobile units on continuous patrol.

Morrow had been a husky, handsome, and popular forty-three-year-old veteran of World War II and had lived in Presidio County since 1931. Under the sheriff's body, investigators found a wallet containing a photograph of a couple dancing in one of Ojinaga's nightclubs. On the back was the name "Jose Villalobos." The officers assumed Villalobos was handcuffed because there were no handcuffs in the car. They also thought that another man, Juan Carrasco, accompanied Villalobos.

The posse began their search Monday morning, tracking Villalobos west of Highway 67 through rough terrain, over mountains, and into canyons through the Jimmy Livingston ranch. Bloodhounds were of no use because the land was so dry. Juan Ochoa, an expert tracker from Presidio, picked up the signs first, and they followed Villalobos into a goat camp seven miles north of the river. Goat tracks erased any further signs. If the near-freezing temperatures made travel on horseback uncomfortable for the posse, the trail showed that Villalobos was not having an easy time of it either. Signs showed that he had fallen many times in his scramble toward Mexico.

In addition to the mounted posse, authorities searched with airplanes, cars, and jeeps with drivers unsuccessfully trying to help, according to some officers. Police also set up roadblocks on all highways leading out of the Big Bend.

Mexican officers cooperated in every way, and when two men near the Rio Grande said they had seen a bloody, scratched-up man going across the river into Mexico, Mexican officers took over. Witnesses said the fugitive was headed through the mountains west of Ojinaga for the small village of Cuchillo Parado, where his mother and sister lived.

Carlos Chavez of the Mexican State Police; Mack Tarwater, deputy sheriff; and Calvin Darst, head of Immigration at Presidio, went back to Presidio, got a four-wheel drive, and sped to cover the seventy miles to the village before Villalobos got there. Two Mexican rangers joined them. Despite their best efforts, Villalobos beat them to the village and came running out of his mother's house when the officers drove up. He halted when they yelled at him. He was bloody, full of stickers, ragged, and exhausted. He wore no handcuffs, but he did have Morrow's gun. He confessed to the killing, saying there was a scuffle when Morrow asked him about his citizenship papers, papers which bore their own bizarre story.

Villalobos had bought Juan Carrasco's citizenship papers from Carrasco's mother for one hundred pesos after Juan died. Under that name, Villalobos had registered for the draft in the United States in 1940 in

Fort Davis. He was twenty-two years old and had worked at one time with Carlos Chavez, one of the arresting officers, in Chihuahua City, Mexico.

When the men returned to Ojinaga, the Mexican officers put Villalobos in the Ojinaga jail, refusing to let him be taken to the United States. They did not allow the American officers to take a written statement from him or talk with him further.

Some Trans-Pecos citizens waited outside the jail and one was allowed to go inside and peer through the tiny opening in the cell door. Villalobos refused to talk, but the man described the jailed man as being slender, with curly dark hair and beautiful green eyes. The American citizen asked to remain anonymous even in 1991.

Juan Ochoa, leaning against an adobe wall, watched the armed American officers talking with other Americans. He saw their unmistakable anger and called a man over to him. "You'd better get these men back across the river, and now," Ochoa said.

The Americans looked around them and suddenly noticed that about a hundred Mexican men had silently gathered in the streets. The Mexicans were not going to let the gringos take their man across to the United States. The situation grew tense. One reporter for *Life Magazine* had his camera confiscated. The Americans, though as familiar with Ojinaga, Mexico, as with the Big Bend, realized they were on foreign soil. Reluctantly they left town and returned to Presidio-- except for a few who forgot that the international bridge closed at midnight. They spent the night in

Ojinaga but left as soon as the bridge opened the next morning.

Mexican law had no provision for turning over nationals to another country for trial. Border officials told American authorities that if Mexican officers became convinced of Villalobos's connection with the crime, they would just "push him across the border" to simplify the matter. Some Mexican officers did indeed plan to smuggle the accused across the river, but the news leaked out and they backed down on the idea.

Because Villalobos did not mysteriously appear on the American side of the Rio Grande, authorities realized they would have to send a formal request through channels: from the sheriff to the governor's office, to the United States Department of State, and to the United States Embassy in Mexico City. From there the request would go first to the Mexican Foreign Office, then to the attorney general, and finally to the president of Mexico. A Mexican rancher promised to work behind the scenes to expedite the return of the wanted man, and American officers thought he could "pull the right strings."

In the meantime, a friend of the Villalobos family secured two injunctions: one, to keep him in the Ojinaga jail, and two, within a few days to move him to Chihuahua City. The Americans never did get Villalobos back for trial. They had launched the biggest manhunt in the history of the Trans-Pecos-- between fifty and seventy-five men had worked for a week, covering five hundred square miles of land, to no avail. The last they heard about him was a few years later. He had been in several movies made in Mexico City.[11]

The court term of Alan Fraser had been far from routine. It was the time of postwar adjustments with people moving about the country trying to settle again into civilian jobs and a civilian way of life, a time of the baby boom and the "new look" in women's clothes. The Trans-Pecos adjusted to the closing of the airfield and army posts. Hopes soared for the good life to come.

Judge Fraser was elected to the Eighth Court of Civil Appeals in El Paso in November 1952. His campaign covered twenty-two West Texas counties, and he succeeded Judge C. R. Sutton on the appeals court. Sutton retired January 1, 1953.[12]

Governor Allan Shivers appointed J. C. Epperson of Alpine to replace Fraser on the 83rd bench. Fraser had served for five years. Epperson would have only until June 5, 1954--seventeen months.[13]

J. C. Epperson
Courtesy of Jean Epperson Glascock

Chapter 6

Wrong Time to Die–J. C. Epperson

John Cleveland Epperson was remembered by his children as a kind, considerate man. A favorite memory was when the family drove along in two touring cars on a vacation in the 1920s. Epperson suddenly slammed on the brakes, jumped out of the lead car, and ran wildly across the freshly plowed black soil of East Texas to throw himself into the arms of the plowman. They laughed and cried as they hugged--the black man and the white man who had grown up together.[1]

Epperson made one mistake in his life: He picked the wrong time to die.

Born in Tyler, Texas, on July 6, 1888, he read law in the office of Cone Johnson and Jim Edwards of Tyler. In 1916 he was admitted to the State Bar of Texas with the highest grade in his group of would-be lawyers. After service in World War I, he went to Edinburg, opened a law office, and became county attorney, district attorney, and county judge in succession. He went into private practice with A. W. Cameron, an association which lasted fifteen years.

Hired to help clear up titles to land in what became the Big Bend National Park, he moved to Alpine in 1942. At the conclusion of that work, he opened his own law office in Alpine.[2] Epperson was appointed to the 83rd on December 14, 1952, by Governor Allan Shivers when Judge Fraser moved to the Court of Civil Appeals in El Paso.[3]

Down in South Texas, politics were building to a boil, erupting in the spring of 1954 over a grand jury. The district judge was ousted by the Texas Supreme Court, and A. S. Broadfoot was appointed as acting judge. He dismissed the old grand jury and began impaneling a new one.[4] Attorneys filed motions to disqualify Broadfoot and to stop the impaneling. With all the political upheaval, the court docket stacked up, and Judge Epperson was asked to go to Alice to help clear out the cases.

While Broadfoot struggled with the grand jury, Epperson heard cases all week in Alice and Rio Grande City. On Friday night, he had a massive heart attack and died early Saturday morning on June 5, 1954.[5]

When the grief and shock began to ebb in the Trans-Pecos over the loss of Judge Epperson, political maneuvering exploded because the Democratic primary election was scheduled for July 24, 1954, and the June 7 filing deadline was past. Epperson had filed for the judge's race before he went to Alice but had not paid the filing fee. E. B. O'Quinn, a Marfa lawyer, had filed and paid his filing fee but was accused of not sending the report of his campaign expenditures by the May 25 deadline, which would invalidate his filing. W. A. Hadden Sr. of Fort Stockton asked that his name be on the ballot but later withdrew the request, claiming to be a candidate for a write-in vote.

The attorney general of Texas now entered the fray, saying it was mandatory for Epperson's name to be on the ballot if the filing fee were paid by anyone by June 26. A friend of Epperson's paid. The other candidate, O'Quinn, asked for mandamus action to get a court ruling that his name should be the only one on the ballot. Word came from Austin that E. B. O'Quinn had filed his campaign expenses in time.

The six Democratic chairmen were in a state of complete confusion. H. M. Fennell of Presidio County refused to put Epperson's name on the ballot. Mary Ann McCormick, secretary to the Democratic chairman of Upton County, decided to wait for court action on the matter. Barry Scobee, Jeff Davis County, and Rolland Sanders, Reagan County, thought both Epperson and O'Quinn should be on the ballot. The Pecos Democratic chairman, W. A. Hadden Jr., was noticeably silent. An attorney from the eastern part of the district, careful to be anonymous, said there was no provision for a write-in candidate in a primary because the primary was a private party election paid for by those who filed in the regular manner.

On July 1, 1954, the Court of Civil Appeals in El Paso spoke, ordering Fennell, the Presidio County Democratic chairman, to put the dead man's name on the ballot. O'Quinn asked the Texas Supreme Court to review the Eighth Appeals Court ruling. It refused, thus endorsing the ruling. Both candidates' names appeared on the ballot. W. A. Hadden Sr. campaigned for the dead man, and W. A. Hadden Jr. resigned as Pecos County Democratic chairman to help his father.

The Pecos County Bar Association passed a formal resolution urging people to vote for Epperson and to attend precinct and county Democratic conventions "to help secure the most qualified judge." Governor Allan Shivers tactfully said he would wait until after the primary to appoint someone to fill the unexpired term of Judge Epperson.

The final days before the election were filled with frantic political campaigning by everyone over the six counties. The dead man won the primary, which was tantamount to a victory in the general election in November. The decision of whose name would appear on the November ballot then went to the Democratic Executive Committee--the Democratic chairmen of the six counties in the district.[6]

The second judge of the 83rd, retired Appellate Judge C. R. Sutton, appeared in Alpine to talk with Gene Hendryx, Brewster County chairman. "He was," Hendryx said, "the most politically knowledgeable man I have ever known. He knew all about Texas politics." The two men wanted the new judge to come from the western part of the district. One Marfa lawyer turned down the offer because he felt he did not have enough experience. They eventually decided on an Alpine lawyer. The committee met in Fort Davis because there were no lawyers residing in the county. Barry Scobee chaired the meeting.[7]

As the chairmen gathered at the Jeff Davis Courthouse on Friday, July 30, 1954, at 2 p.m., so did several men interested in the outcome--E. B. O'Quinn; Warren Burnett of Fort Stockton, who was interested in W. A. Hadden Sr.; and others. Rumors had it that threats had been made against the chairmen. After the six filed into a room, Texas Ranger Arthur Hill closed the door, pulled up a chair, and sat down, eyeing the crowd. They got the message.

Those present were Gene Hendryx of Alpine, Brewster County; Barry Scobee of Fort Davis, Jeff Davis County; Jones Taylor of Fort Stockton, Pecos County; H. M. Fennell of Marfa, Presidio County; Rolland Sanders of Big Lake, Reagan County; and L. E. Windham of McCamey, Upton County. Scobee was elected chairman; Hendryx, secretary.

A tally of votes in the primary election held July 24, 1954, was presented by each chairman, giving Epperson, the dead man, 4,474 votes and O'Quinn, 2,921 votes. By a majority of 1,553 votes, Epperson was officially declared the nominee.

There followed heated debate over the candidates, but the final outcome was for C. E. Patterson of Alpine, with a vote of 4 to 2, to be the nominee on the November ballot.

When the results were announced to the waiting crowd in the hall, tempers flared. One man ran into the room cursing, but the Ranger soon calmed him. Patterson immediately resigned his position as county attorney of Brewster County. Bruce Sutton, son of C. R., was appointed to that job. Governor Shivers appointed Patterson to finish Epperson's unexpired term.[8] Court could now get back in session.

J. C. Epperson's term of office was brief, but as interesting as his predecessors' had been. He was missed, but the chairmen had chosen well. C. E. Patterson was to remain as judge for nearly eighteen years until he left as Epperson did, and another political to-do took place.

However, in September, Barry Scobee, Jeff Davis Democratic chairman, sent Della Bond, Presidio County district clerk, a notarized copy of the formal action because Fennell said he did not have a copy. Scobee asked that she return the copy because he wished to keep it as a "souvenir of the first such nomination probably ever made in Texas."[9]

C. E. Patterson
Courtesy of Archives of the Big Bend, Bryan Wildenthal Library,
Sul Ross State University, Alpine, Texas

Chapter 7

The Baseball Judge–C. E. Patterson

"He kept up over the years with all the children whose adoptions he handled. Those were his favorite cases," said Hallie Patterson, Judge C. E. Patterson's widow.[1]

"A bluff, hearty man."[2]

"He knew all the best restaurants in West Texas."[3]

"Pat loved baseball, and that got him into trouble once."[4]

His ability to get along with people shook up a Dallas lawyer when Judge Patterson admonished a West Texas lawyer in court with "Don't say that."

"Okay, Pat," the lawyer agreed.

"Too familiar," the Dallas attorney said with a frown.

It took a few seconds for the Trans-Pecos people and the judge to figure out what might be wrong.[5]

The new judge was born in Florence, Texas, in Williamson County on September 17, 1905. After

attending Southwestern University at Georgetown, he
went to Baylor University at Waco for his law degree.
His father owned two farms in the rich Central Texas
farmlands, but there was no ready cash. Pat worked at
three jobs in Waco: at the dorm for a place to live, at
Luby's Cafeteria for a place to eat, and at a dry
cleaner's for cash. He collected students' clothes, took
them to the laundry, and returned them.

When asked when he studied with this busy
schedule, he answered, "Every chance I had."

"But when did you sleep?"

"Seldom."

He had the ambition and drive necessary for his
success in both education and law. He and Hallie Davis
of a pioneer family of Presidio County married on July
30, 1931, and he began practicing law with W. W. Van
Sickle of Alpine the same year. He was county
attorney for twelve years before becoming district
judge in 1954.[6]

The judge's love of baseball got him into trouble
with a Reagan County jury. It was on Monday,
October 8, 1956. The jury had been recessed for lunch,
and the judge, stocked up with lunch meats, crackers,
and cheese, moved in front of the television set. Bob
McLaughlin, court reporter; Lucius Bunton, district
attorney; and a few others joined him to watch the
World Series being played between the Dodgers and
the Yankees--until 1 p.m. when the jury had been told
to return to the courtroom.

When the six-foot-four pitcher, Don Larsen, passed
the 1927 record of Herb Pennock's retiring twenty-two
men in succession, all 64,519 baseball fans in the

stadium came roaring to their feet. Plus a few in Big Lake, Texas. Any thought of returning to the courtroom was simply silly.

Larsen pitched the perfect game, the Yanks winning 2-0.

When the happily grinning men trooped back into the courtroom, they were met by a silently threatening, angry jury and a few dour officials.

It took the judge's profuse apologies plus promises that tomorrow they could watch the game too before the jury consented to resume their labors.7

But not all was fun and games in Judge Patterson's court. The Vaught murder trial of 1960 held the rapt attention of the entire 83rd from the small village of Presidio on the Texas-Mexican border in Presidio County, where the shooting occurred, to Rankin, the county seat of Upton County, where the trial was held.

It was not your usual doctor-to-patient house call in Presidio. In front of Herman West's white picket fence, Dr. Clyde Vaught, sixty years old, shot and killed H. E. Dupuy, seventy-six, owner of the Presidio-Ojinaga International Bridge. He used a rifle that late afternoon of October 2, 1959.

"I didn't know what else to do. I thought he was pulling a gun on me," Vaught explained in a shaky voice to the standing-room-only Rankin courtroom--to Judge Patterson, the jury, court officials, school children from Rankin and McCamey, local citizens, and people from Marfa and Presidio.

The gun was a 44-40 caliber rifle Vaught tossed into the back seat of his car with his medical kit as he left home to go to the West house. Several people had warned him to be wary of Dupuy, and Dupuy had threatened him.

Dupuy was sitting on the front porch of the Starr Hotel. He watched Vaught drive by and followed in his own car, burning rubber in the gravel as he pulled into the street. Dupuy stopped the vehicle a few steps from Vaught's car, and Vaught said he shot the man.

When officers emptied Dupuy's coat pocket, they found an eight-inch by three-fourth-inch chisel. No gun.

After the Presidio County grand jury indicted Vaught for murder with malice on October 17, 1959, the trial was moved to Rankin, 160 miles away, where people were not so emotionally involved. The trial began on April 4, 1960.

Prosecutors for the state were Warren Burnett of Odessa, Steve Preslar of McCamey, John R. Florence of Kilgore, and District Attorney Norman Davis of Marfa, the judge's brother-in-law. Defense attorneys were Brian Montague of Del Rio, John Menefee of McCamey, and W. H. Earney and H. O. Metcalfe of Marfa. Quite a battery on both sides.

Courtroom dramatics kept the spectators engrossed. One witness, Ernest Williams of Marfa, a large man, lunged from the witness stand with doubled-up fists and shouted at veteran attorney Brian Montague, "You ought to learn how to examine witnesses!"

It took three officers to force him from the courtroom.

The trouble between Vaught and Dupuy began many years earlier in Presidio. Vaught had been county commissioner of Precinct 3, which included Presidio, for ten years. Dupuy had asked him several times for the use of county equipment to repair roads leading to the international bridge following Rio Grande floods.

Vaught refused, considering that as private, not county, business. Dupuy became angry.

His bridge had been a bone of contention over the years. After hearing reports of floods in Presidio, the first question many people asked was, "Did the bridge go?"

When the bridge toll rates were raised by both Mexico and Dupuy, Presidio businessmen organized to protest to the U. S. Army Corps of Engineers in Albuquerque, New Mexico. They said many Ojinaga people could not afford the new rates to get to Presidio and the stores were hurting, losing revenue.

However, the Corps of Engineers set the toll rates charged by privately owned international bridges between the United States, Mexico, and Canada.

Vaught attended several of the businessmen's meetings, and Dupuy thought the doctor was heavily involved in the protest. Dupuy turned down an offer of $50,000 by the Presidio businessmen to buy the bridge.

Newspaper accounts depict Dupuy as a troubled, unhappy man. One Presidio citizen became so frightened by Dupuy's threats that he left town.

During the trial, H. M. Lovelady, Marfa and Presidio businessman, quoted Dupuy as saying, "I have lived in Presidio a long time, and I take what I want."

It was said that Dupuy became angry with a bill collector and chased him around his car until Dupuy's son, Frank, could stop him.

As he grew older, Dupuy became more troubled. Three days before the shooting, Dupuy is reported to have called Vaught and said, "I'm coming to Presidio to shut you up."

Vaught told this to Presidio County Sheriff Ernest Barnett, who advised Vaught to stay home and be careful. Others warned Vaught to look out.

The jury was deadlocked, reheard four hours of testimony, and acquitted Vaught. [8]

Of added interest, on the night of the shooting two businessmen from Odessa were driving toward Marfa and wrecked their car on a tricky curve across the bridge, immediately north of Presidio. A. T. "Tommy" McCall, deputy at Presidio, in a car with DA Lucius Bunton and County Attorney Bill Earney drove to the wreck.

At the scene, one man was sitting beside the road holding his head and moaning. He looked up at McCall and said, "Don't tell my wife. Don't tell the officers, and get me a doctor."

McCall broke the news gently. "Sorry, son, but I am the law. This is the district attorney, this is the county attorney, and the only doctor within sixty miles has just been arrested for murder."

Judge Bunton later recalled that McCall was "an old Big Spring boy and a friend of George Cross. It was Deputy McCall who took Bill and me around and showed us where the killing took place, and we interviewed some witnesses.

"We were having coffee around 8:30 or 9:00 o'clock on O'Reilley Street when somebody came in and told Deputy McCall there had been a wreck at the bridge. We went in my car to the bridge, and these two drunk fellows had indeed failed to make the curve and had run through the fence. One of them had his nose hit by the windshield and it broke his nose. . . .

"The end of that story was that we were in my new 1959 Ford, and Bill and I brought these two fellows back from Presidio, and the fellow with the broken nose bled all over my back seat. I never did get all of that blood out, even until the time when I traded the car in 1965. We took these two fellows who had wrecked their pickup to the Paisano Hotel, and they checked in the next morning with Sheriff Ernest Barnett."9

But murder was not the only issue to keep the interest of people in West Texas. Land is the lifeblood of the Trans-Pecos economy, and in this ranching and oil west, land cases stirred emotions. Three land cases during Judge Patterson's era were of special note. Two involved the Davis Mountains State Park, and one hearing concerned, basically, the odd question of who owns the rain clouds over the land.

There was so much fussin' and feudin' over the case of the Texas State Parks Board vs. Willie Merrill and Tom Gray that Mrs. Merrill wrote, "I wish the State Parks Board (sic) would move out (of the Davis Mountains State Park) so (sic) the old eyes, old cows, and all humans could sit down and rest."

Four years later she wrote, "I've . . . called Mr. Collins [Bill M. Collins, executive secretary of the State Parks Board, Austin, Texas] an old Son of a Buck (sic) right to his nice face. . . . I told the poor man that and I wasn't mad then."

Before it was all over, she was mad.

The trouble began innocently on November 18, 1933, when the state bought from J. W. and R. K. Merrill two hundred acres of land up Limpia Canyon from Fort Davis on the highway to the McDonald Observatory. This was the beginning of the Davis Mountains State Park.

On January 18, 1934, two months later, the two ranchers gave a ninety-nine-year, rent-free lease to the Texas State Parks Board in exchange for an additional 1,340 acres and the reservation of certain livestock grazing rights. In the agreement, a surveying marker was listed as "a lightning blasted old cedar oak tree blazed midway up."

The Merrills gave the land for the "quiet enjoyment" of the public and prohibited any commercial enterprise. The state agreed to make certain improvements. It was a generous gesture on the part of the ranchers.

However, by 1957, Mrs. Willie Merrill, widow of R. K., had inherited the land, and she was unhappy because the given land was in a sad state--unkempt, overgrown roads, and worst of all, her livestock strayed on to the highway because of the poorly kept fences.

The final blow came when she heard about some area people going to a meeting of the Parks Board in San Antonio on May 6, 1957. They said she had fenced off the land, keeping people from getting into the park and using Skyline Drive. Rumor had it that someone wanted a commercial enterprise started there. In August 1957 some of those same people had second thoughts and went back to the Parks Board in Austin asking that their names be removed from the petition. By now Willie was irritated with the entire situation. She locked the gates.

There was a loud uproar in Austin, and a suit was filed for an injunction to make her unlock the gates. On May 10, 1958, Judge Patterson said that the state had not kept its part of the bargain. The Court of Appeals in El Paso upheld him, so the state went to the Supreme Court. The Supreme Court reversed the Court of Appeals and sent the injunction back with instructions for negotiations.

Correspondence between lawyers hinted that an agreement could be reached but recommended that Willie not be present, being the feisty little woman she was. Fate took a hand, assisted by the local doctor who had been cued in. Mrs. Merrill became ill and was under the care of Dr. W. H. Stover of Marfa. Suddenly George Enloe, who worked for the Merrills, generously offered to represent Willie at the negotiations.

She wrote the lawyers that the doctor thought her blood pressure might go up under stress and would the lawyers please excuse her and accept George? They wrote her, assuring her gravely that she would be missed, but they might manage without her.

Negotiating parties agreed that Willie could keep the grazing rights, but she had to give keys to the locked gates to the State Parks Board. In exchange, the state announced certain improvements. Mrs. Merrill, however, had the last say in the matter in letters to her lawyers.

"A good job you and Mr. Kerr [William L. Kerr of Midland] did for me. Don't forget about me. . . . Every time I see a bunch of buzzards (sic) flying around I think of the danblamed (sic) Park Board and old man Wilson [Attorney General of Texas Will Wilson]. . . . I hear Wilson is going to clean up all State officials but (sic) he didn't say who would clean him up."

And in another letter she wrote, "Tell the biggest politician in the State what I said and let him bounce it up and down the hall of justice if he knows where one is.

"P.S. I bet they're holding a prayer meeting for Mr. Espy to die."[10]

J. W. Espy of Fort Davis had locked horns with the Texas State Parks Board over a similar situation to the Merrills'. On June 10, 1957, Espy wired his lawyers that I "want my lease canceled on account of abandonment." The State Parks Board was in for another wrangle.

It began under similar circumstances to the Merrills'. In 1933 J. W. Espy and his wife, Lola Pruett Espy, conveyed in a deed two hundred acres of land to the Parks Board for park purposes with the understanding the state would keep the area in good repair. The land originally had been owned by early settler B. H. Greerson Jr., and Espy acquired it in July 1910.

In 1957 Jim Espy, son of the rancher, locked the gates, and the state filed suit to unlock them.

At the hearing Judge Patterson ruled Espy should get the land back. The state filed an appeal on August 28, 1962. The appeals court upheld Patterson's ruling.

Espy contacted the Parks Board saying, "Now, if you guys will just do what I asked. . . ."

On April 1, 1963, Espy once again gave the land to the state, and this time the state agreed to three specific improvements to begin before January 1, 1966, and to finish before January 1, 1968:

1. Pave the scenic drive and make parking areas.
2. Develop picnic and camping facilities including water, lights, and rest rooms.
3. Keep the park in good repair.

Espy reserved all grazing rights.

However, in November of 1961 the Texas Research League had pronounced the state parks in bad condition, and the board had taken two steps:

1. To set State Parks Board Minimum Standards.
2. For park experts of Texas Tech University to make long-range plans for park acquisitions, interpretation, and maintenance.

In August 1962 the board had approved a new budget, a five-figure sum, for the Davis Mountains State Park to rehabilitate existing facilities. As of the summer of 1996, the Davis Mountains State Park is one of the cleanest, best-kept parks in the state. Not only don't mess with Texas, but especially don't mess with the Trans-Pecos ranchers.[11]

The third case that grabbed the public's attention and fired emotions was one of the first weather-altering cases. Basically it was a question of what right a landowner has in the clouds. Farmers and ranchers must have water to keep their land producing, and in the dry Trans-Pecos, with few lakes and streams for irrigation and scattered windmills, the clouds are necessary for survival.

"Being in the ranching business, when you walk outside, you just naturally look up" at the clouds, the ranchers say. Early settlers marked their routes from rivers to watering places, exchanged shots over water holes, and fought over fences barring access to water. In 1958 they fought in court.

Too much rain or heavy hail damages crops. The Trans-Pecos Cotton Association, made up of Reeves County and Pecos County farmers, decided to hire the Southwest Weather Research, Inc. of Houston to prevent hail in the spring of 1958.

The ranchers of the area had been happy in the fall of 1957 and early 1958 because a long drought was breaking. Rain clouds were forming, but suddenly, in early 1958, they began seeing silver airplanes flying around in their rain clouds. Twenty minutes after the plane passed, there were no clouds.

"It was awful! If we don't get rain, we're in trouble!" said Jim Duncan, who had owned a ranch nineteen miles north of Fort Davis since 1918.

One day as he and his hands sheared sheep, they kept watch over the clouds that were building over Gomez Peak.

"Great thunderheads. Very white. . . . As they come up, they get darker." Out of such clouds come rain.

Duncan watched a small, silver plane fly in and through the thunderheads. He said, "The clouds frazzled out and disappeared."

Willis McCutcheon, rancher, related a similar sight when he worked on a windmill. "It made a fellow feel like he was having a nightmare. I wrote it [what happened and the date] when I could get my nerves steady enough to write . . . in a black notebook. Time after time, I've seen a good-looking cloud just fold up and disappear right after one of them dang airplanes went through it."

The ranchers compared information, organized, and took the case to court, telling the cotton farmers to "leave our clouds alone."

At the end of June 1958, the farmers offered to compromise with the ranchers with a proposal that the farmers and ranchers combine to hire a "recognized and impartial scientific research agency to determine the full facts of the case. The farmers offered to pay half the cost involved." The farmers felt that, by seeding the clouds, damage by hail was avoided and rainfall was increased.

A. F. Buchanan, farmer and member of the Trans-Pecos Weather Control, Inc., said the feud between the two groups was "the bitterest dispute since the Indians attacked the last wagon train out here."

The ranchers remained unconvinced and refused compromise. Suit was filed by July 17.

Two cases were filed but were consolidated for an injunction hearing. The ranchers asked Judge Patterson to stop the cloud seeding. Area people gathered to hear the testimony at the Fort Davis courthouse. Families picnicked on the shady courthouse lawn during noon recess.

William L. Kerr, attorney for the weather research company, said, "It's been the friendliest hostile crowd I've ever been around."

Again the courtroom was full and the news media occupied the jury box. Dave Medley, a forty-seven-year-old rancher, revealed a poetic talent as he described rain clouds. His ranch lay twenty miles west of Fort Davis, some eighty-two hundred acres stocked with cattle. Medley had the look of a typical cowboy, deeply tanned face up to a white hat line on his forehead, work-worn hands, worn but well-polished boots, and blue jeans.

On the witness stand he thought long and hard before answering the lawyer's questions. Yes, a rain cloud had "a big, old, soft head. . . . A rain cloud that will not rain is a hard, broken cloud which is shaggy. . . Everyone looks over [Mount] Livermore for the clouds."

He spoke even slower when asked to describe, in his own words, a rain cloud. He was silently thoughtful before a soft smile lighted up his eyes. He had found the words, and with great relief he said, "They sure are pretty. There's *nothing* prettier than thunder and lightning."

Southwest Weather Research, Inc. used three planes in their cloud-seeding procedures--a BT-13 and two AT-6s. They flew through two potential thunderheads, spewing out dry ice, silver iodide crystals, and salt particles. On the ground were generators doing the same thing. The pilots were Eugene K. Kooser, John Lewis, and Nealy Bingham. Scientists testified, giving detailed analysis on how and why thunderheads develop and rain falls.

George Asa Jones, Fort Stockton rancher, said it simply, "The cowboys say when the wind is blowing into a cloud, it will rain."

Judge Patterson granted the injunction to stop the cloud seeding. The cotton farmers went to the Eighth Court of Civil Appeals at El Paso. The court upheld the district court. They went to the Texas Supreme Court, which upheld the injunction saying, "Weather changes had been hired by a group of cotton farmers in the Fort Stockton area to disperse hail-producing clouds over the Fort Davis Mountains with a chemical. Ranchers claimed by seeding clouds the particles of matter around which water collects and condenses cause the moisture to form in small drops and are forced up in the warm air currents and doing away with the moisture. The injunction was temporary until the complicated scientific problems could be fully considered."

That ended the matter between farmers and ranchers. Little had ever been said about how a farmer feels while he watches his main money crop being beaten down by hail.[12]

Peggy Garner, commissioner of the Texas Water Commission, said that her agency is in charge of regulating "all weather modification (cloud-seeding) activities in Texas through a licensing and permitting process." After it has been proved that a person or group has had "proper experience and expertise," a license is issued. Three areas of weather modification are "rainfall augmentation, hail and/or lightning suppression, and fog dissipation." Notices of intent must be published, and proof of insurability presented.

According to Garner, the Colorado River Municipal Water District, Big Spring, "has been seeding summertime convective clouds . . . virtually every summer since 1970." Research of the Colorado River Municipal Water District has shown that cloud seeding has "given ample evidence that the seeding of convective clouds is linked with substantial increases in rainfall."[13]

The court case on cloud seeding in Fort Davis came during the 1950s "during the worst drought in recorded weather history." The controversy helped lead "the Texas legislature to enact legislation on weather modification a decade later."

Then death came unexpectedly to Judge Patterson. He suffered a heart attack at his home on June 27, 1972.[14]

There had been many changes during his seventeen years and ten months of service. The Trans-Pecos suffered a drought. The economy improved in the 1960s. The people sent their sons and husbands to Vietnam. The favorite songs from the era went from "Davy Crockett" and "Sixteen Tons" to "Blue Suede Shoes" and "If I Were a Rich Man" from *Fiddler on the Roof.*

The Cuban Missile Crisis, the assassination of John F. Kennedy, space exploration--television brought all these events into people's living rooms all over the world, including the Trans-Pecos. The African-American community was protesting, organizing, and beginning to make progress in schools. The Hispanic community was stirring politically.

Judge Patterson had just won the June Democratic primary election. As in 1954 with the death of Judge Epperson, Democratic politics heated up over who would be the candidate on the November general election ballot. Party activists had been through this before in 1954, and they knew what to do.

William H. Earney, 1973

Chapter 8

The Affable Judge--William H. Earney

"God willin' and the creek don't rise" is a West Texas saying. Unfortunately, the creek did rise, and J. R. "Red" Patillo was behind high water in the Big Bend National Park while the other five Democratic Party county chairmen gathered in Fort Stockton to cast their ballots for the new judge of the 83rd.

Patillo found a back road, and leaving a heavy, dusty cloud, managed to arrive in Fort Stockton before the group proceeded without him. With a one-vote majority, William H. Earney, district attorney of the 83rd, was to be the candidate in the November election. Several days later Governor Preston Smith called the Earney home.

"Mrs. Earney, this is Governor Smith."

Since West Texas people like to play practical jokes, she answered sarcastically, "Really?"

"I like to tell the wives first," the governor said.[1]

During a newspaper interview, the new judge was asked why he had chosen a law career.

Earney answered candidly. "Way back in 1936 when I looked up at the sky from a twelve-foot hole that was to become part of the Greyhound bus station in Austin, it was at least 115 degrees. I put down my shovel and vowed no more ditch digging and lots more education."

Born in Belton, he graduated from Abilene High School, put himself through the University of Texas at Austin, then took four years out to serve in the U. S. Navy during World War II. He returned to law school in 1950, received his degree in the spring of 1954, and moved to Marfa, where he rose through the legal ranks: veterans' service officer, city attorney, county attorney, district attorney, and district judge. He worked in the law office of Hunter O. Metcalfe. That small office with three lawyers turned out three judges: State District Judge Metcalfe, Federal District Judge Lucius Bunton, and Earney.[2]

The new judge provided some interesting courtroom drama during a land case in Fort Davis because he never wore a judicial robe.

"I'm so short," he explained with a twinkle in his eyes. "If someone told me to stand up while I was wearing a robe, I'd already be standing."

When he impaneled a jury, he always told the members that if they needed to take time out during the proceedings, to signal him and he would excuse them for a few minutes. During a well-attended land case in Fort Davis, the jury had signaled and signaled, but the judge ignored them. They did not know that he whispered to Sheriff Wid McCutcheon to telephone the police dispatcher in Marfa with a message for his wife. "But don't put it on the Trans-Pecos radio!"

The message was, "Bring me my other pair of pants."

The Baptist preacher who had been contacted entered the back of the courtroom with a choir robe over his arm, and the judge shook his head. Finally his wife arrived. McCutcheon, grinning widely, cleared the courtroom much to the disgust of the spectators. When the judge stood, his trousers fell off neatly in two pieces. A vital seam had ripped.

After the trial the next day, a conversation was overheard between two Fort Worth lawyers as they walked down the wide steps of the Jeff Davis Courthouse.

"They aren't going to believe this back home [the city]. One of the witnesses brought his own spittoon, and the judge lost his pants!"

A grateful jury presented the judge with an elaborately wrapped present--a sewing kit.[3]

Of more sober consideration was the murder trial in Fort Stockton of Alvaro Hernandez Jr. in January 1976. He was accused of killing Robert A. Beard, age twenty-one, a clerk at the Ramada Inn, in Alpine in September 1975. Events surrounding the trial got out of hand, and rumors flew that the accused was going to kill the only witness, who had turned state's evidence. As the witness testified, alerted law enforcement personnel seated around the courtroom kept a watchful eye. The brittle silence was broken by a metallic clatter in the back of the courtroom. Leather slapped. A child wailed. He had dropped his toy car.

When the noon break came, the judge decided to walk across to the Fort Stockton Library (in the old building) and get some silence and rest. As he sat at the table leafing through a magazine, he became aware of two things. The library had grown unusually quiet, and the sound of a running motor filled the air. He glanced up and saw that everyone had left the building except the librarian and a rancher, who leaned against the counter. They were both watching him. Realizing that the sound of the motor was growing louder, the judge glanced down--into the face of a mountain lion, switching its tail and purring contentedly.

"I'll swear that cat was smiling," the judge said later.

It was a pet, and the rancher liked to take him to town to visit.[4]

Back in the courthouse, the jury found Hernandez guilty, and Earney ordered him held in Fort Stockton's new jail until he could be transported to the Texas penal system at Huntsville. According to the newspapers, during the night, two trustees managed to overpower the guard in charge, and the newly sentenced man and three other inmates gathered a handy amount of guns and ammunition, took a car from the jail parking area, and headed southwest for Mexico. Two hours later, around midnight, the relief guard came to the jail and found the hapless guard locked in a cell. He immediately issued an all-points bulletin.

With the coming day, the United States Border Patrol got involved, and they located the four fugitives across the Rio Grande in Mexico. With full cooperation between Mexican and American law enforcement personnel, the four were caught between the river and the semicircle of armed men. A shootout began. One of the escapees dead-sighted a sheriff, but the gun jammed. Following the surrender, the men were returned to jail with additional charges lodged against them.[5]

In November of 1976 the gun did not jam, and Sammy Charles Long, eighteen-year veteran of the Texas State Highway Patrol, died with eleven gunshot wounds--six from his own service revolver and five from a .32 caliber weapon.

A San Angelo hunter and his son had stopped at a roadside park three miles east of Rankin as had two young girls, students at San Angelo State University. A muddy green pickup with California license plates roared into the park at high speed followed by a highway patrol car with lights flashing.

The four at the roadside park watched in horror as the patrolman approached the pickup, and the driver came out firing a .32 caliber weapon. Long, the policeman, ran behind his car and fell. The stranger from the pickup pulled the patrolman's gun from its holster and fired into his back.

The hunter reacted and grabbed his 6mm deer rifle, aimed, and fired at the pickup driver, killing him and saving the lives of the witnesses. The girls immediately got on the CB and called for help.

There was instant cooperation among law enforcement personnel, other state patrolmen, the district attorney, and the news media. The names of the four witnesses are still held in confidence.

Aubrey Edwards, district attorney, was quoted as saying, "The hunter attempted to save the life of the patrolman when he fired his rifle. It's something that absolutely wouldn't happen again in a thousand years. Absolutely no charges will be filed."

To repeat a phrase: Don't mess with Texas.[6]

Don't mess with my sense of justice, Judge Earney declared in another case. Mario Hurtado went to work one morning on an oil rig, and one split second changed his life. An oil pipe smashed into his back, leaving him a C-6 quadriplegic, permanently paralyzed from the neck down.

In Case #4236, Pecos County, a trial was held at the Fort Stockton courthouse after his lawyer refused a million dollar settlement offered by the Ron Ric Corporation.

The jury awarded Hurtado $289,000, less than the corporation lawyers had asked for in their closing arguments to the jury. Hurtado's lawyers asked for a mistrial and Earney granted it.

The corporation immediately went to the Eighth Court of Civil Appeals in El Paso, asking that Earney be compelled to "sign, render, and enter" a final judgment based on the jury's decision.

The Court of Appeals upheld the "judicial discretion of the Court." You could almost hear the judge give a sign of relief from Fort Stockton to El

Paso. An award of a much greater amount was finally given the young man from Mexico.[7]

The most difficult murder trial Judge Earney heard was the one involving the murder of Hank Hamilton, the Presidio County sheriff and Earney's good friend. The case was transferred to Fort Stockton in Pecos County.

Hamilton was elected sheriff in November 1972 and took office in January 1973. On April 27 he was called about a parked car on the Ralston Road, two miles west of Marfa. Tommy Vaughn, Ralston ranch hand, had seen the white 1965 Olds and stopped to talk with the driver about two o'clock the afternoon of April 27, asking him to leave. Vaughn reported the man to ranch foreman Gratton Taliaferro, who notified the sheriff.

Hamilton and Deputy William Massey drove out to investigate. Hamilton never drew his gun but was shot five times as he tried to talk with the driver.

After the shooting, Massey could not get to his car to use the radio. He ducked behind a nearby water tank before running down the road to the highway, stopping a highway department truck. The driver took him to Marfa, where he reported the incident to the Border Patrol.

Within minutes, Thomas J. Henderson of Marfa, a longtime pilot with the Border Patrol; Robert Walker, chief Border Patrol pilot; and Robert Williams Jr. flew over the scene, Williams acting as observer.

Area law enforcement, including Texas Ranger Arthur Hill, assisted with the investigation.

Narciso Sanchez, Presidio County justice of the peace, held George S. Duckworth, fifty-one, on $200,000 bail.

The grand jury two weeks later indicted Duckworth on a count of murder with malice plus attempted murder of Deputy Massey. The accused was sent to the Ector County jail in Odessa until the trial in Fort Stockton.

According to Aubrey Edwards of San Angelo, 83rd Judicial District attorney at that time, Duckworth was a retired major of the U. S. Air Force, having served for twenty-two years. He had spent his retirement years living out of his car and driving around the United States, tape recording everything he did. He had a tape playing when Hamilton approached his car. Hamilton's dying gasps were played in court.

Both the judge and the district attorney said the entire trial was difficult and emotional for them because of their friendship with Hamilton, but there was never any question of bias during the proceedings on the part of the court.

Since the superior court had outlawed the death penalty, Duckworth was given a life sentence. However, he died in a nursing home about ten years later.

Duckworth had said he had no funds to pay for a defense attorney, but Edwards said it was later found he had a solid bank account and was in no way indigent. [8]

Judge Earney continued to hold court until 1984 when he retired.

If it were not for the funny happenings in court, officials would be grim individuals indeed. Earney recalls the time a witness was asked to name his church preference. The prompt reply was "red brick," which caused some chuckles. "Obviously a Methodist church," the judge said.

On the grimmer side was the convicted killer who said as he was being led away from the courtroom, "If I had a B-52 loaded with bombs, I'd know where to drop them."

The district attorney, Aubrey Edwards, and the judge pointed at each other instantly and said simultaneously, "He means you."

Another accused murderer offered a memorable statement when asked why the dead man had been shot in the back. He said, "The bullet must have gone around him."

Then there was a bridge player who constantly interrupted the game to denounce the jury system and its leniency on criminals. However, after serving on a jury, she became apologetic saying, "It's a lot different when you're on the jury than when you're a spectator."

Earney remembers being called "Sonny Boy" by an Alpine woman lawyer during his first days in court, being dubbed "Porky Pig" in a half-page advertisement in the Marfa newspaper, and being called a good judge when he retired. He shrugged and grinned. "It is nice to be promoted."[9]

Judge Alex Gonzalez became judge in 1984, the first Hispanic to serve as a judge of the 83rd.

Alex R. Gonzalez

Courtesy of Archives of the Big Bend, Bryan Wildenthal Library,
Sul Ross State University, Alpine, Texas

Chapter 9

First and Last—Alex R. Gonzalez

"I have come into the picture at a new era when most of the seasoned attorneys are retiring. As a result, I have a young breed of attorneys with little experience making it much more difficult in trying cases. In the past most lawyers loved the practice of law and wanted to help people. The motivation is different now. Some attorneys want to help, but most don't," Judge Gonzalez remarked on the changing times. He said he wanted to "encourage, not discourage" the young people.

However, he came in at just the right time.[1]

The Hispanic people were becoming more active politically, and Gonzalez was the first Hispanic appointed to the district as judge. He had behind him many years of experience with foreign governments, leaving him most able to deal with any cases involving Mexico. He had been in the U. S. Navy for four years after graduating from Fort Stockton High School.

During his four years in the service he acted as Spanish interpreter for his officers in Argentina, Peru, Panama, and Uruguay. He found this assignment ironic because he had been spanked in public schools for speaking Spanish on school grounds.

He was assistant to Congressman Richard White in Washington, D. C. and later White's liaison officer working out of Austin. He was also an executive officer with the Peace Corps in Peru for two years.

Woven in and out of these activities was his formal education--Sul Ross State University, the American University in Washington, D. C., and the University of Texas Law School. All of this was capped by a successful law practice in Fort Stockton. His pioneering ancestor, Saturno Gonzalez, who settled in the Fort Stockton area in 1869-1870, would have been very proud of him.[2]

Gonzalez was the right man at the right time, but he became the last judge of the six-county 83rd Judicial District of Texas. He was appointed by Governor Mark White in February 1984. Michael Rodgers, Dallas lawyer and attorney for the Rio Grande sniper, said, "He [Gonzalez] was impeccably fair. He knew his stuff. He didn't allow anyone to get away with any foolishness."[3]

At least two interesting cases involved some action in Mexico during Gonzalez's term: the case of the Rio Grande sniper and the case of "barbed wire justice" instead of hang-and-shoot.

In November of 1988 Michael Hefley, forty years old and from Eastland, Texas, wanted to show Jamie, his wife of thirteen years, the Big Bend National Park.

They were both avid outdoors people, enjoying camping, hiking, and exploring. This time they were taking the popular Colorado Canyon river float trip with Jim Burr, thirty-six, of Terlingua, Texas, and an experienced river rafter guide.

The adventurers put into the river twenty-two and a half miles up river from Lajitas.

In Mexico at the same time, as fate would have it, four angry young men were gathering in the rough countryside. One, Eduardo Pineda Rodriguez, was a Mexican citizen living in the United States on an alien amnesty program. He stayed with his parents in Redford, a tiny village sixteen miles southeast of Presidio in the United States.

Border Patrol agents said over the past few years there had been several reports of shots being fired from Mexico into United States territory.

The men were a short two miles from the Hefleys' launch site, watching the river some three hundred feet below.

Jamie Hefley noticed smoke rising from the canyon top and almost instantly bullets began spraying the water around their raft. A .22 caliber bullet punctured Burr's thigh, but he was able to get the raft to the American side of the river. The rafters quickly decided to go down river to a spot where brush would give them some cover. Bullets continued falling.

Near the brush they began scrambling on to a sand bank when Jamie was hit in the shoulder. Her husband threw himself over her to protect her, trying to reach brush, when he was shot in the back with a .30-30.

Within a few minutes Michael died with Jamie and Burr crouching over his body.

From midmorning until dark, the two stayed there. Burr slipped out of the brush after dark and made his way to FM Road 170, but it was not until the next morning that a Presidio farmer came by and picked him up. Jamie had spent the night in 30-degree weather crouched in the brush.

The night before by 9:30 p.m., the owners of Far Flung Adventures, the rafting company, were worried and started looking for the three missing persons. It did not take them long to discover the bullet-riddled raft and equipment. They immediately contacted the Brewster County sheriff, who, in turn, contacted the Presidio County sheriff. By 8 o'clock the next morning the Border Patrol and the U. S. Immigration Service had helicopters out searching the river. Both spotted Hefley's body about the same time. As they went in to Hefley, Jamie staggered out of the brush. She was immediately flown into Alpine to the hospital. Burr was taken there also.

West Texas law enforcement went to work-- Presidio County's sheriff, Rick Thompson; anti-drug smuggling agents of the U. S. Border Patrol; U. S. Immigration agents; and people from the Texas Parks and Wildlife Department, Texas Department of Public Safety, and even the Texas Cattle Raisers Association. The Chihuahua State Judicial Police cooperated wholeheartedly.

As a result, two teenagers were arrested by December 1--Eduardo Pineda Rodriguez, seventeen, at Redford, and a sixteen-year-old boy at El Mulato in

Mexico across the Rio Grande from Redford. The latter was locked in the Ojinaga jail. Pineda Rodriguez was charged in Marfa with murder and attempted murder. Two others were being sought in Mexico.

Judge Gonzalez heard the case in Presidio County, and Pineda Rodriguez was sentenced to thirty years in jail. His lawyers appealed, arguing that the judge erred in allowing evidence of the arrest of the accused on immigration violation charges and certain evidence found at the Redford home during the search, including the murder weapon--a rifle.

It was a sticky point. Because Pineda Rodriguez was living in the United States on a permit, federal officers got an immigration search warrant from a federal magistrate in Pecos after hearing he had re-entered the United States without telling anyone. Under the circumstances, of course, he was not about to tell anyone. Thus he had entered illegally. He also admitted taking part in the shooting with two other people who lived at El Mulato. According to his statement, there had not been four shooters although trackers stated they saw four different sets of tracks.

At a pretrial hearing to suppress the search warrant and the evidence found, the judge ruled to allow the evidence to be used and the search warrant valid.

The appeals court upheld his ruling. Always good news to a judge.[4]

The barbed wire incident happened because Brewster County residents were mad this time.

The newspaper reported that down near Terlingua in Brewster County, a Mexican national had crossed over the river and broken into a house where a woman lived alone. He held her at knife point all night, assaulting her repeatedly. He then returned to Mexico but was arrested by Mexican police as he made his way to San Carlos, Mexico.

The constable was nervous about releasing the man, Refugio Ardea Gonzales, to Texas law officials, so he handcuffed the man to a truck mirror and held him there all day. Finally the constable took him to the Ojinaga jail. It was announced that he would be tried in Mexico.

That did not set well with some Brewster County men. They went across the river at night and dragged Ardea Gonzales out of jail, bound him, gagged him, and brought him back to a roadside park near Alpine. They left him gagged, blind-folded, and half-naked-- bound to a tree with barbed wire. When the sheriff finally found him and pulled off the gag, the man began screaming, "Mafioso! Mafioso!" (Mafia! Mafia!).

Then it got interesting. The sheriff said he did not know who called him to tell him of the prisoner's location or who had brought the man out of Mexico. Mexico had not complained about the incident. The underworld boss in Ojinaga protested he knew nothing about it. Billy Pat McKenney, constable, said someone got paid off. Rumor had it that guards at the jail and two Hispanics and one Anglo were the vigilantes. All in all, a mysterious affair.

Judge Gonzalez had the case transferred to San Angelo on a change of venue.[5]

In 1995 the boundaries of the old 83rd were changed by the Texas legislature. Some felt with the growth in population and increase in crime that the work load was too hard on one judge. Representative Pete Gallego from Alpine introduced the bill, and the legislature passed it.

Brewster, Jeff Davis, and Presidio Counties were taken out of the 83rd and put into a new 394th Judicial District along with Culberson and Hudspeth Counties. These last two counties are on the west side of the 83rd. All cases pending in the 83rd were transferred to the 394th effective September 1, 1995.

Kenneth D. Dehart of Alpine was appointed as the first 394th district judge of the new five-county alignment. Judge Gonzalez continued as judge of the 83rd. The new 83rd consisted of Reagan, Upton, and Pecos Counties.[6]

There is much more rich history in the years of the six-county 83rd. Only a part has been discussed here. With the growing population and "outsiders" moving in, who knows what changes will come, but as of 1997 lawyers were still representing friends and neighbors. West Texas witnesses and jurors were still educating new, young lawyers in the ways of the Trans-Pecos country.

ENDNOTES

Map

1. Supplement to Vernon's Texas Civil and Criminal Statues, Vol. 1, Civil Statutes, Titles 1 to 67A; Kansas City, Mo: Vernon Law Company, 1918, p. 43, Section 83.

2. General Laws of the State of Texas Passed By Thirty-Ninth Legislature At Its Regular Session Which Convened January 13, 1925, and Adjourned March 19, 1925, p. 84, Chapter 24, Section 83.

3. General Laws Of The State Of Texas Passed By The Forty-First Legislature At The Second And Third Called Sessions; The Second Called Session Convened At Austin, Texas, June 3, 1929, And Adjourned July 2, 1929, The Third Called Session Convened At Austin, Texas, July 3, 1929, and Adjourned July 20, 1929. The State of Texas: Jane Y. McCallum, Secretary of State, pp. 246, 247, Section 3. Reaffirmed, General And Special Laws Of The State of Texas. Passed By The Regular Session Of The Fifty-Third Legislature, Convened At The City of Austin, January 13, 1953, And Adjourned May 27, 1953. Authority Of The State of Texas: Howard Carney, Secretary of State, pp. 393, 394, Chapter 109, Section 1, Subdivision 83.

4. Texas Judicial Report, Office of Court Administration, Texas Judicial Council, Legislative Edition, July 1995, p. 1; Legislative

Information System 74(R), Bill Text Report, HB 3235, Enrolled
Version, LI8030C, p. 5, Section 20, Amendment Section 24.539, p.
5; *Big Bend Sentinel,* 5 October 1995.

Chapter 1

1. Bill Bunton, interview, Marfa, Texas, 2 June 1983. Bunton was a
   Presidio County rancher, whose family was among the first settlers
   of Presidio County.

2. "Brewster County," "Jeff Davis County," "Pecos County," "Presidio
   County," "Reagan County," "Upton County," *Texas Almanac,
   1976-1977.*

3. John Fletcher Earney to Marvin Corder, Marfa, Texas, June 1957.

4. The author was there.

5. Many West Texas lawyers make these two statements.

6. Wayne Gard, *Frontier Justice* (Norman: The University of
   Oklahoma Press, 1949), pp. 6, 7.

7. William Ransome Hogan, *The Texas Republic: A Social and
   Economic History* (Norman: The University of Oklahoma Press,
   1946), pp. 245, 246.

8. Clifford Casey, *Mirages, Mysteries, and Reality: Brewster County,
   Texas. The Big Bend of the Rio Grande* (Hereford, Texas: Pioneer
   Book Publishers, 1972); Clayton W. Williams, *Texas's Last
   Frontier. Fort Stockton and the Trans-Pecos, 1861-1895*, ed. Ernest
   Wallace (College Station: Texas A&M University Press, 1982), pp.
   1-323; Celia Thompson, *History of Marfa and Presidio County,
   Texas, 1535-1946*, Vol. 1 (Austin, Texas: Nortex Press, 1985), pp.
   1-304; James Harwood Lundy, master's thesis, "History of Jeff
   Davis County," Sul Ross State University, Alpine, Texas, 1941.

9. Gard, *Frontier Justice,* pp. 11, 21.

10. See note 8.

11. *Fort Stockton Pioneer*, 11 May 1917.

12. H. O. Metcalfe to author, circa 1960.

13. Pecos County Civil and Criminal Minutes, 1, 15.

14. Conversations with H. O. Metcalfe.

15. Judge Lucius D. Bunton, telephone conversation with author, circa November 1978.

16. William H. Earney, early 1960s.

17. See note 1.

18. C. M. "Fritz" Kahl, telephone conversation with author, September 1997.

Chapter 2

1. Hollis Haley, interview, Alpine, Texas, 14 May 1985. Haley was a rancher in the Sanderson-Marathon area.

2. *San Angelo Standard Times*, 1 March 1937.

3. Pecos County Civil and Criminal Minutes, III, p. 221.

4. *Fort Stockton Pioneer*, 10 May 1918.

5. *Alpine Avalanche*, 5 January 1921, 16 February 1921, 1 July 1921, 21 July 1921, 7 October 1921, 24 December 1921; *San Angelo Daily Standard*, evening edition, 20-26 June 1921, 15-19 November 1921; Val Verde County District Court Minutes Book, 5, pp. 25, 51, 71; Case #945, Val Verde Case File; Case #945, Val Verde County District Clerk's Office, Del Rio, Texas.

6. Mrs. J. E. White Sr., telephone interview, Marfa, Texas, 2 February 1983.

7. William H. Earney, Marfa, Texas, 1970s.

Chapter 3

1. *Alpine Avalanche*, 3 June 1941.

2. James Weatherby, interview, Big Lake, Texas, 24 April 1991.

3. Mrs. P. B. Croom, letter to author, 3 May 1985.

4. Dr. C. R. Sutton Jr., letter to author, 3 October 1983; *Alpine Avalanche*, 3 January 1941; *The New Era*, 6 February 1922, 17 February 1922; "Sutton," Ellia A. Davis and Edwin H. Grobe, *The New Encyclopedia of Texas* (Dallas: Development Bekreae, no date, circa 1951), also p. 2090.

5. *The New Era*, 10 March 1923; *Alpine Avalanche*, 12 February 1922, 19 October 1922, 26 October 1922, 4 January 1923, 15 February 1923, 1 March 1923, 8 March 1923, 12 April 1923; *Fort Stockton Pioneer*, 9 March 1923; "Toronto," *The Handbook of Texas, II* (Austin, Texas: The Texas State Historical Society, 1952).

6. *San Angelo Daily Standard*, evening edition, 19 May 1923, 28 May 1923, 3 June 1923, 4 June 1923, 6 June 1923, 8 June 1923, 10 June 1923, 11 June 1923.

7. *San Angelo Daily Standard*, evening edition, 4 October 1925, 6 October 1925, 18 October 1925, 22 October 1925, 23 October 1925, 25 October 1925; *Fort Stockton Pioneer*, 9 October 1925; *Big Lake Wildcat*, 2 October 1925, 10 October 1925, 12 December 1925; Juror's Time Book, #1, Reagan County District Court Clerk's Office, Big Lake, Texas, 34; Criminal Minutes District Court, I, Reagan County, pp. 28-74; Criminal District Court Jackets, Case #66, Case #1163, filed 23 October 1925, 1 August 1925; *The New Era*, 23 July 1927, 6 August 1927.

8. *Fort Stockton Pioneer*, 9 March 1928, 16 March 1928, 8 June 1928.

9. James Weatherby (Weatherby said the Ranger's name was Charles Curie); *San Angelo Standard Times*, 7 June 1934, 9 August 1934; file, Presidio County District Clerk's Office; Miss Billie Harper, Miss Mary Lee Harper, interview, Marfa, Texas, May 1991 (they were longtime residents of Marfa); T. D. Wood, interview, Marfa,

Texas, May 1991 (Wood is a rancher in southern Presidio County); the author attended parts of the trial.

10. *Big Bend Sentinel*, 27 January 1939; H. O. Metcalfe conversation, February 1939; Charles Shindler to author, Marfa, Texas, circa November 1944.

11. *Big Bend Sentinel*, 31 December 1937.

12. *Big Bend Sentinel*, 2 February 1940.

13. *Big Bend Sentinel*, 21 August 1940, 30 August 1940, 8 November 1940; *Alpine Avalanche*, 3 January 1941.

14. *Big Bend Sentinel*, 17 January 1941.

Chapter 4

1. *Big Bend Sentinel*, 17 January 1941; *Alpine Avalanche*, 17 January 1941; John Fletcher Earney, "Hunter Orgain Metcalfe," research paper, *Marfa Junior Historian*, 1968; Metcalfe family files; *San Angelo Standard Times*, 29 January 1957.

2. *Big Bend Sentinel*, 17 January 1941; *Alpine Avalanche*, 17 January 1941.

3. *El Paso Times*, 16 August 1941; 1957 newspaper feature (month and date unknown), author's files; H. O. Metcalfe, interview, Marfa, Texas, 1957; Fox Parker Jr., interview, Marfa, Texas, 1957; Presidio County District Court Minutes, pp. 45-51, *Big Bend Sentinel*, 13 August 1941, 20 August 1941; Metcalfe family files.

4. *Fort Stockton Pioneer*, 12 September 1941.

5. *Fort Stockton Pioneer*, 18 October 1946.

6. *Alpine Avalanche*, 19 December 1947.

Chapter 5

1. *Alpine Avalanche*, 1 September 1944.

2. Alan R. Fraser, letter to H. O. Metcalfe, 5 January 1945.

3. *Alpine Avalanche*, 3 August 1945, 19 December 1947; *Big Bend Sentinel*, 19 September 1947; *Texas Bar Journal*, clipping dated 1953, no month, in author's files.

4. *Alpine Avalanche*, 19 December 1947; *Big Bend Sentinel*, 19 December 1947.

5. *Big Bend Sentinel*, 30 January 1948; *Fort Stockton Pioneer*, 30 January 1948.

6. *Fort Stockton Pioneer*, 3 September 1948.

7. See note 11.

8. H. O. Metcalfe, letter to Brian Montague, 24 March 1950.

9. James A. Porter Jr., *Doctor, Spare My Cow* (Ames, Iowa: The Iowa State College Press, 1956, pp. vii-xii); "Brucellosis," "Foot-and-Mouth Disease," *Encyclopedia Americana,* 1992 edition; Dr. C. W. Edwards, veterinarian, interview with author, Marfa, Texas, 20 July 1991.

10. Carter "Buck" Newsome, interview with author, Marfa, Texas, 22 July 1991; Earl Lankford, interview with author, Marfa, Texas, 20 July 1950; *Big Bend Sentinel*, 20 January 1950, 27 January 1950, 3 February 1950; *Alpine Avalanche*, 20 August 1948, 18 February 1949, 19 February 1949, 26 August 1949, 2 September 1949, 27 January 1950, 3 February 1950; newspaper clippings, H. O. Metcalfe files, "Babb Case," dateline 29 January 1950, 31 January 1950; Case #1462, files of the Presidio County District Clerk's Office, Marfa, Texas; Minutes District Court, I, Presidio County Courthouse, Marfa, Texas, pp. 235, 247-253; H. O. Metcalfe, letter to Brian Montague, 3 February 1950.

11. *Alpine Avalanche*, 17 March 1950; *Big Bend Sentinel*, 17 March 1950; *Fort Stockton Pioneer*, 17 March 1950; *El Paso Times,* 13-19

March 1950; *San Angelo Evening Standard*, 13-17 March 1950; Marfa citizen, interview, name withheld on request, on file in author's notes, 15 July 1991.

12. *Alpine Avalanche*, 1 February 1952, 1 August 1952; *Fort Stockton Pioneer*, 28 July 1952, 31 December 1952.

13. *Alpine Avalanche*, 19 November 1952.

Chapter 6

1. Jean Epperson Glascock, daughter of J. C. Epperson, letter to author, May 1983.

2. Glascock; *Alpine Avalanche*, 10 June 1954.

3. *Fort Stockton Pioneer*, 18 December 1952, 25 December 1952; *Alpine Avalanche*, 19 December 1952.

4. *San Angelo Evening Standard*, 1 June 1954, 4 June 1954, 6 June 1954, 10 June 1954; *Alpine Avalanche*, 11 June 1954.

5. *Alpine Avalanche*, 11 June 1954.

6. *Alpine Avalanche*, 25 June 1954, 2 July 1954, 30 July 1954, 6 August 1954; *Big Bend Sentinel*, 10 June 1954, 24 June 1954, 1 July 1954, 8 July 1954, 29 July 1954; *Fort Stockton Pioneer*, 10 June 1954, 24 June 1954.

7. Gene Hendryx, Brewster County Democratic chairman in 1954, interview with author, Alpine, Texas, 26 June 1991.

8. Name withheld on request, on file in Earney notes, July 1991; *Alpine Avalanche*, 6 August 1954; minutes of a meeting held in Fort Davis, Texas, Jeff Davis County, 30 July 1954, by the six Democratic county chairmen of the 83rd Judicial District.

9. Barry Scobee, letter to Della Bond, 28 September 1954. Letter in files of Mrs. Clay Miller, Valentine, Texas, Democratic chairman for Jeff Davis County in 1991.

Chapter 7

1. Hallie Davis Patterson, interview, Alpine, Texas, 1985.

2. William H. Earney, interview, Marfa, Texas, June 1991.

3. Gene Hendryx, interview, Alpine, Texas, 26 June 1991.

4. Bob McLaughlin, interview, Alpine, Texas, 26 June 1991. McLaughlin was court reporter for the 83rd for many years.

5. McLaughlin.

6. Patterson, interview, circa 1969, Alpine, Texas.

7. *El Paso Times*, 9 October 1956; one baseball history book had the date of 1957; McLaughlin; Federal Judge Lucius Bunton, interview, Lajitas, Texas, 1991.

8. *San Angelo Standard Times*, 9 April 1960, 13 April 1960; *Midland Reporter Telegram*, 10 April 1960; *Big Bend Sentinel*, 1 October 1959, 9 March 1960, 31 March 1960; newspaper clippings with no dates from Rankin, *San Angelo Standard Times*, *Odessa American*, H. O. Metcalfe files; Presidio County Criminal Docket, 12, p. 429; Case #381, District Clerk's Office, Rankin, Texas, Upton County Courthouse.

9. Lucius Bunton, letter to author, 8 May 1995.

10. State of Texas v. Willie Merrill and Tom Gray, Case #907, Jeff Davis County Clerk's Office, Fort Davis, Texas; Willie Merrill, letters to H. O. Metcalfe, 12 July 1957, 22 July 1961, 18 September 1961, 7 October 1961; H. O. Metcalfe letters to Frank D. Quinn, Austin, Texas, 6 June 1957, to Bill M. Collins 5 May 1957, to Jim Glasscock 6 May 1958, to Quinn, Texas State Parks Board member, 2 July 1957, to William L. Kerr, Midland, Texas, 24 July 1957, to Willie Merrill 31 January 1961; letter to Metcalfe from Judge Richard Critz and F. L. Kykendall, no date, from Bill Collins, 3 July 1957, from William L. Kerr, Midland, 24 July 1957, 22 April 1960; *Alpine Avalanche*, 5 May 1968; *Big Bend Sentinel*, 16 August 1962; Texas Supreme Court, Case No. A-7665, State of Texas v. Willie

Merrill and Tom Gray, 20 April 1960; lease J. W. Merrill and R. K.
Merrill to the State of Texas, January 18, 1934, Vol. 33, p. 620,
deed records of Jeff Davis County, Fort Davis, Texas; *Odessa
American*, circa 21 November 1961; *Southwestern Reporter*, 2d.
Series, Texas, pp. 432-435, State of Texas Petitioner v. Willie
Merrill, a Feme Sole, and Tom Gray, Respondents; Metcalfe and
W. H. Earney files.

11. J. W. Espy, telegram, 10 June 1957, to H. O. Metcalfe; General
Warranty Deed, Deed Records, #61, pp. 640-641, Jeff Davis
County Clerk's Office, Fort Davis, Texas; Case #924, District Court
files, The State of Texas v. J. W. Espy; Jeff Davis County Clerk's
Office, Fort Davis; *Big Bend Sentinel*, 16 August 1962; Earney and
Metcalfe files.

12. William Walter McElroy Jr., testimony; Jim Duncan, testimony;
Willis McCutcheon, testimony; *West Texas Livestock Weekly*, San
Angelo, Texas, 12 June 1958; Dave Medley, testimony; Jim
Duncan et al. v. Southwest Weather Research, Inc., Case #916, Jeff
Davis County Clerk's Office, Fort Davis, Texas; *El Paso Herald
Post*, 3 May 1958; Southwest Weather Research v. Jim Duncan et
al. #5351, October 15, 1958, Eighth Court of Civil Appeals, El
Paso; *Southwestern Reporter*, Texas Supreme Court No. A-7201:
Southwest Weather Research, Inc., et al., v. Jim Duncan, et al.; *Big
Bend Sentinel*, 7 August 1958; clippings, *San Angelo Standard
Times*, no date, Earney and Metcalfe files; *San Angelo Standard
Times*, 1 July 1958; *Fort Stockton Pioneer*, 26 June 1958.

13. Peggy Garner, Texas Water Commission, Austin, Texas, letter to
author, Marfa, Texas, 10 August 1993.

14. *Alpine Avalanche*, 29 June 1972.

Chapter 8

1. *Fort Stockton Pioneer*, 3 August 1972, 10 August 1972; J. R. "Red"
Patillo, interview, Alpine, Texas, 1992; Mrs. Clay Miller, interview,
Marfa, Texas, 1992. Patillo was Brewster County Democratic
chairman and Mrs. Miller was Jeff Davis County Democratic
chairman at the time of Judge C. E. Patterson's death.

2. William H. Earney conversations; *San Antonio Express*, 1 August 1972.

3. *Fort Stockton Pioneer*, 3 August 1972; *Alpine Avalanche*, 3 August 1972; Earney family files.

4. Earney family files.

5. The State of Texas v. Alvaro Hernandez Jr., #1234, Pecos County District Clerk's Office, Fort Stockton, Texas; *Alpine Avalanche*, 18 September 1975, 18 December 1975, 25 December 1975; *El Paso Times*, 19 December 1975, 25 January 1976; *Fort Stockton Pioneer*, 21 December 1975, 18 January 1976, 22 January 1976, 15 February 1976; *San Angelo Standard Times*, 25 January 1976, 8 August 1976; *Odessa American*, 13 January 1976; Earney files. From Huntsville, Hernandez wrote a letter published in the *Alpine Avalanche* December 17, 1981, maintaining his innocence.

6. *San Angelo Standard Times*, 22 November 1976; *Midland Reporter Telegram,* 22 November 1976; *Odessa American*, 23 November 1976.

7. Joint Answer to Relator's Petition for Writ of Mandamus; No. 08-83-00081-CV, Ron Ric Corporation, Relator, vs. The Honorable William H. Earney, Respondent, Mario Hurtado, Real Party in Interest, 3 May 1983; interviews, William H. Earney, spring and summer 1983, Marfa, Texas.

8. *Big Bend Sentinel*, 19 July 1973; interview with William H. Earney, 1970s; interview with Aubrey Edwards, 1970s and 1994, Marfa, San Angelo, and Big Lake, Texas.

9. Earney conversations; Earney files.

Chapter 9

1. Judge Alex R. Gonzalez, interview with author, Marfa, Texas, circa September 1990; *San Angelo Standard Times*, 27 January 1990.

2. Gonzalez; *Alpine Avalanche*, 11 April 1972, 9 December 1993; *Fort Stockton Pioneer*, 17 February 1972.

3. *San Angelo Standard Times*, 27 January 1990.

4. *Alpine Avalanche*, 24 November 1989, 1 December 1989; *Big Bend Sentinel*, 24 October 1991.

5. *Big Bend Sentinel*, 11 August 1986; Walt Harrington, "The Last Days of the Lawless West," *The Washington Post*, 6 April 1986; Case #2422, State of Texas v. Refugio Ardea Gonzales, Presidio County District Clerk's Office, Alpine, Texas.

6. Legislative Information System 74 (R), Bill Text Report, HB 3235 Enrolled Version, June 1, 1995, Section 20, courtesy Representative Pete Gallego; *Big Bend Sentinel*, 23 March 1995, 18 May 1995; Texas Judicial Report, Office of Court Administration, Texas Judicial Council, Legislative Edition, July 1995, pp. 1, 2, 17.

.

Index

About the Author

Born and raised in Marfa, Texas, Mary Katherine Earney grew up in a family of storytellers and writers. In addition, she heard her father, Judge H. O. Metcalfe, and his friends discussing their court cases as she would later hear her husband, Judge William H. Earney, and his friends discuss theirs.

With a B. A. in history from the University of Texas at Austin and a master's degree in history from Sul Ross State University in Alpine, Texas, she taught social studies for ten years in Marfa Elementary School. She became special correspondent and photographer from the Big Bend area for El Paso, San Angelo, and Fort Worth newspapers, covering stories from federated teas to bull sales to historical interviews.

She had four children.

Her other books are *Woolgathering*, a compilation of her weekly columns for the *Big Bend Sentinel* covering social history of growing up in a small West Texas town, and Volume II of the autobiography of Dr. Francis Asbury Mood, a nineteenth-century circuit rider who later became the first regent of Southwestern University in Georgetown, Texas. She is currently editing the letters of 1921-1926 river riders and Volume III of Dr. Mood's life.